hands-off
cooking

hands-off cooking

Low-Supervision,
High-Flavor Meals
for Busy People

ann martin rolke

1807
WILEY
2007

BICENTENNIAL · BICENTENNIAL · BICENTENNIAL

JOHN WILEY & SONS, INC.

Interior design and layout by Renato Stanisic
Interior and cover illustrations © Beth Adams

Published by John Wiley & Sons, Inc., Hoboken, New Jersey
Published simultaneously in Canada

For general information about our other products and services, please contact our Customer Care Department within the United States at (800) 762-2974, outside the United States at (317) 572-3993 or fax (317) 572-4002.

Wiley also publishes its books in a variety of electronic formats. Some content that appears in print may not be available in electronic books. For more information about Wiley products, visit our web site at www.wiley.com.

Library of Congress Cataloging-in-Publication Data:

Rolke, Ann Martin.
  Hands-off cooking : low-supervision, high-flavor meals for busy people / Ann Martin Rolke.
     p. cm.
  Includes index.
  ISBN   978-0-471-75681-1 (pbk.)
  1. Quick and easy cookery. I. Title.
TX833.5.R65 2007
641.5'55--dc22

Printed in the United States of America

10 9 8 7 6 5 4 3 2 1

Acknowledgments

A million thank yous go to Laurie Abkemeier, my agent, without whom this book would never have been cooked up. Her experience and tact were invaluable and she was definitely hands on!

Thank you to the many, many friends and neighbors who came to "guinea pig" nights and tasted recipes as they were developed. Your feedback and company kept me on track. Special thank yous to my recipe testers and sounding boards: Leslie Hawkins, Tatiana Graf, Ari Branson, Cyndi Wreford, Michelle Baass, Crista Martin, Margaret Martin, and Judy Rolke.

Thank you to the team at Wiley: Justin Schwartz, for believing in the project; Ava Wilder, for working with me on this as well as many other books; and Carolyn Miller, fellow copyeditor, for her keen eye and great queries.

And last, but never least, thank you to my husband, Bob, for happily tasting, shopping, brainstorming, and eating his way through this book process. I'm a lucky girl indeed, to have found someone so bacon-compatible!

contents

Introduction:
The Secret to Impressing People and Regaining Your Sanity

You race around all day, pick up the kids or dry cleaning, or both, and arrive home once again to face that den of *inequity*—the kitchen. It's just not fair that you should have to deal with providing a healthy, budget-conscious, and appealing dinner after the day you've just had! What you need is some *Hands-Off Cooking*.

Hands-off cooking is not a new concept—people around the world have practiced it for centuries. From spit-roasted meats to slow-simmered stews, our ancestors have counted on dishes that can cook unattended while they deal with the other necessities of life. Since they didn't have take-out as available as we do, they planned ahead a bit and multitasked.

On weeknights, you may want to choose recipes that require a shorter cooking time. On weekends or holidays, make recipes like Carolina Pulled Pork (page 108) that require a few hours of cooking but still allow you to relax and enjoy some down time while making a terrific meal.

Modern hands-off cooking is made easier by the multitude of partially prepared whole foods now available. Look at the refrigerated section of your grocery's produce department: You'll find shredded carrots, diced onions, and peeled cubes of squash. The meat department has precooked chicken and precut beef for stir-fry. There are also shredded cheeses, freshly canned fruits and vegetables, and dozens of frozen ingredients ready to use.

Take time to familiarize yourself with what your local stores offer. You don't need to rely on high-sodium and preservative-laden packaged foods to get dinner on the table quickly. You may even find that you save money by not buying packaged foods and take-out all the time. And you'll surely be eating more nutritious meals.

Hands-off recipes are also ideal for entertaining. Because they need little attention while cooking, you won't be answering your door with spatula in hand and food-spattered party clothes. What an enviable host you'll be when your guests arrive to find you calmly sipping a glass of wine with your feet propped up!

The Basics

Hands-off recipes have a relatively short prep time followed by unattended cooking. That means no turning, adding ingredients, or stirring the food. You can walk away while it cooks—just don't forget and leave the house.

The prep time for all of these recipes varies significantly, depending on your swiftness in the kitchen, your organization of equipment, and whether you use partially prepared ingredients. Make use of those prechopped and frozen vegetables; gather all of your ingredients so they're ready to add; and have the cooking implements you need close at hand. When you've made a recipe once, you'll find that it goes faster the next time you put it together.

The hands-off time listed at the beginning of each recipe indicates the unattended time—including any marinating, cooking, and resting periods—that you'll have to do other things. You may notice that the cooking techniques are slightly different than usual. In order to ensure real hands-off cooking, I developed ways of making recipes so that you don't have to sauté, stir constantly, or otherwise watch over the food as it cooks. For instance, many hands-off stove-top recipes begin at a low temperature and cook for a bit longer than if you brought them to a boil and then had to reduce the temperature. Likewise, several meat recipes begin with heating a pan with oil until it is shimmering, and then you add the meat and leave it to brown while you prepare the other ingredients. When you add the remaining ingredients, you reduce the heat so that the food cooks unattended from then on. Look for the Hands-Off Technique notes throughout the book to highlight some of these methods.

These recipes take their flavors from cuisines around the world. With so many ethnic restaurants and ingredients now available to us, and one of the most diverse populations in the world, Americans have come to love a variety of foods. Fortunately, a larger ingredient pantry means we can do more with a few basic cooking techniques. For example, with one soup pot you can make Indian Aloo Cholay (page 54), Cajun Gumbo Rapide (page 34), Scandinavian Pea Soup Ann (page 44), and Chinese Gingerrific Chicken Soup (page 38).

Even if you just have a few basic ingredients—I always have onions, minced garlic, and canned tomatoes on hand—you can make many of the recipes in this book. The choice is yours whether to buy things like prediced onions or to buy whole onions and dice them yourself. The deciding factor may be cost (the whole will be cheaper) versus time (the prediced will be faster to use). I tend to use a combination of prepared ingredients and fresh whole additions.

You'll also save yourself some time by doing large batches of some prep and storing the rest. For example, when toasting nuts, toast a whole pound and then store them in the freezer to prevent them from getting rancid. Similarly, you can grind up several stale heels of bread and store them in a heavy-duty plastic bag in the freezer for bread crumbs whenever you need them. I even use a food processor to chop up several onions at a time if I'm going to be doing a lot of cooking in a day or two (perfect for holiday time!).

You'll find Hands-Off Techniques, Stress Savers, and Eye Appeal tips throughout the book to make your cooking as easy as possible and just as attractive as more hands-on meals. Once you get the hang of hands-off cooking, you may wonder why you spent so much (or little) time in the kitchen before! Enjoy the process—cooking is a wonderfully nurturing thing to do for yourself and those you love.

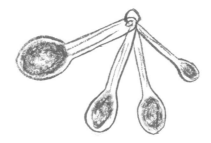

ingredients

Following are some of the pantry items and time-saving pieces of equipment that will make your kitchen more hands-off and less time-consuming. If you make one big trip to stock up every couple of weeks, you'll only need to replace items as you use them, but you should always have something that can be useful. If you have a particular ingredient to use up, check the Index (page 173) for ideas.

Pantry

Dried pasta

Couscous

Quinoa

Baby (new) potatoes

Diced canned tomatoes—I buy a 12-can case at a big-box store

Canned beans: garbanzo (chickpeas), black, pinto

Canned diced green chiles

Dried fruit

Dried thyme, oregano

Ground ginger, cinnamon

Paprika, cayenne, ground chiles (in addition to chili powder)

Chicken or vegetable broth

Olive oil: pure and extra-virgin

All-purpose flour

Yellow or white cornmeal and polenta

Sugar: white and light or dark brown; look for self-sealing bags to preserve freshness

Baking powder

Baking soda

Kosher and sea salt—I developed all of the recipes using kosher salt. If you use table salt instead, you'll need about half as much as the amounts listed (instead of 1 teaspoon kosher salt, use 1/2 teaspoon table salt).

Peppercorns in a grinder

Refrigerator

Garlic: minced or crushed, in a jar; peeled whole cloves

Ginger: crushed, in a jar

Eggs or egg substitute

Milk, soy milk, or rice milk

Shredded cheeses

Ground or boneless, skinless chicken and turkey

Citrus fruit

Roasted bell peppers

Sun-dried tomatoes (the new soft kind, or oil-packed)

Unsalted butter

Freezer

Sliced fruit and berries

Nuts: whole and sliced or chopped

Unbaked pizza dough

Bread crumbs, dried

Extra unsalted butter

Prep-Ahead Items to Save Up When You Have Extra Time

Toasted nuts: freeze (see page 151)

Bread crumbs: freeze

Diced onions: refrigerate in an airtight self-sealing plastic bag

Tomato paste: put 1 tablespoon in each compartment of an ice cube tray; freeze and seal in an airtight bag

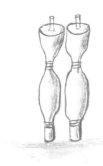

Equipment

There are two kinds of equipment: basic and time-saving. If you're just starting to assemble a kitchen, at least aim for the basic items. With a little ingenuity, you can make practically any recipe with a bare-bones kitchen arsenal.

Bare Bones

5-to 7-quart pot with lid—preferably an ovenproof set (no plastic handles)
10- or 12-inch sauté pan or skillet with lid
9 × 13–inch baking pan or casserole
Set of dry measuring cups, including 1 cup, 1/2 cup, and 1/4 cup
Set of measuring spoons
Large mixing bowl
Pot holder or kitchen towel
Heatproof spoon in wood, silicone, or metal (a silicone spatula is very versatile)

Sharp 8- to 10-inch knife, preferably good quality
Cutting board in wood or composite plastic
Can opener (get one with a bottle opener on it too)

Next Step

Kitchen timer: one that times more than 1 recipe
Strainer (or use a coffee filter)
2-cup liquid measure
2-quart casserole
10-inch pie plate
Serrated knife
Paring knife or vegetable peeler

Metal offset spatula with a cutting edge

Additonal cutting boards

Rolling pin (or use a wine bottle)

Whisk (or use a table fork)

Meat thermometer

Oven thermometer

Rimmed baking sheet (jelly-roll pan), or use
    heavy-duty aluminum foil

Cheese grater

Everything but the Kitchen Sink

Mandoline

Food processor

Blender

Citrus juicer

Pastry brush

Zester

Spice grinder or coffee grinder

hands-off  cooking

salads & sides

Two Cucumber Salads

HANDS-OFF:
30 MINUTES

Here are two versions of a quick cucumber salad. You'll be surprised at how different they can taste with minor ingredient changes. I like to use the long "seedless" cucumbers. Although they still have some seeds, these are easily scraped out using the tip of a spoon.

SERVES 6

2 large seedless cucumbers
   (about 2 pounds)
1 cup thinly sliced red onion

Asian Version
1/4 cup white wine vingar or
   rice vinegar
1 tablespoon sugar
1 teaspoon salt
1/2 teaspoon red pepper flakes

Greek Version
1/4 cup red wine vinegar
1 tablespoon sugar
1 teaspoon salt
1/2 cup (2 1/2 ounces) crumbled
   feta cheese

1. Slice the cucumbers in half lengthwise, then scoop out the seeds using the tip of a spoon. Cut the halves into thin (1/8- to 1/4-inch) slices. Put them in a large nonreactive bowl with the onion.

2. For either version: In a small pot, heat the vinegar, sugar, and salt over low heat just until the sugar dissolves. For the Asian version, add the red pepper flakes and pour the mixture over the cucumbers. For the Greek version, pour the mixture over the cucumbers and then add the feta. Toss the salad well and refrigerate it for at least 30 minutes for the flavors to come together. Stir once more before serving.

Red Cabbage Slaw

Fresh red cabbage, carrots, and red bell pepper make for a colorful salad that has a light dressing. If you can find preshredded cabbage in the refrigerator section of your produce department, it will cut your prep time even more. Make a big batch of this refreshing salad to keep on hand during hot weather. It's great with the Carolina Pulled Pork (page 108).

SERVES 6 TO 8

3 tablespoons freshly squeezed lime juice

1 1/2 teaspoons sugar

3/4 teaspoon freshly ground black pepper

3/4 teaspoon salt

1/2 teaspoon ground coriander

One 10-ounce bag shredded red cabbage, or 1/2 small head, shredded (about 3 1/2 cups)

2 cups shredded carrots

1/2 red bell pepper, very thinly sliced (about 2/3 cup)

1/2 cup thinly sliced scallions, including green parts

1. In a large bowl, whisk together the juice, sugar, pepper, salt, and coriander. Add the vegetables and toss them well to coat with the dressing.

2. Refrigerate the slaw for at least 20 minutes for the flavors to come together. Serve cold or at room temperature.

Bread Salad

**HANDS-OFF:
15 MINUTES**

Bread salad is a classic Italian dish to use up slightly stale bread. I like to use small balls of fresh mozzarella called bocconcini or ciliegine. They have a soft, fresh flavor that pairs well with the garlicky bread and acidic burst of the cherry tomatoes. If you happen to have a grill going, lightly grill the bread instead of toasting it. The smoky essence will add just that much more flavor.

SERVES 4

Four 3/4-inch slices crusty, wide
   Italian bread, such as black olive
   or pugliese
1 clove garlic, peeled and halved
8 ounces fresh mozzarella balls,
   drained
2 cups cherry tomatoes, halved
   if large
1 cup chopped fresh parsley
2 tablespoons extra-virgin olive oil
1 tablespoon balsamic vinegar
Salt and freshly ground black
   pepper to taste

1. Toast the bread well in a toaster or broiler (or on the grill). Immediately rub each piece on both sides with the garlic. (Discard any garlic that remains, but I usually use the whole clove.) Then cut the bread into 3/4-inch cubes.

2. If the mozzarella balls are larger than the cherry tomatoes, halve or quarter them.

3. In a large bowl, combine the bread cubes with the mozzarella, tomatoes, parsley, oil, vinegar, and a sprinkle of salt and pepper. Toss everything well and then let stand for 15 minutes at room temperature to combine the flavors. Toss again and serve.

Eye Appeal: Look for containers of multicolored cherry tomatoes to add interest to the salad.

Roasted German Potato Salad

I love German potato salad, with the salty taste of bacon and the tang of vinegar, but it takes a few steps to put together. In this version, roasting the potatoes makes them crisp while rendering the bacon at the same time. This is delicious with Perfect Pot Roast (page 106) or Garlic-Roasted Chicken with Orange (page 116).

HANDS-OFF:
30 MINUTES

SERVES 6 TO 8

2 pounds red or yellow baby (new)
    potatoes (1- to 2-inch diameter)
1 cup diced red or sweet yellow
    onion, such as Vidalia or Maui
2 tablespoons olive oil
1 tablespoon whole-grain mustard
1/2 teaspoon salt
1/2 teaspoon freshly ground
    black pepper
1/3 cup distilled white or apple
    cider vinegar
4 slices bacon, diced

1. Preheat the oven to 425°F. Lightly oil a nonreactive rimmed baking sheet (jelly-roll pan).

2. Cut the potatoes into wedges and toss them in a large bowl with the onion, oil, mustard, salt, and pepper. Spread them onto the baking sheet in a fairly even layer, scraping all of the mustard seeds out of the bowl onto the potatoes. Pour the vinegar over the potatoes. Scatter the bacon evenly over the top.

3. Bake for about 30 minutes, or until the potatoes are fork-tender and the bacon is somewhat crispy. Serve the salad warm, mounded in a large bowl.

Raita (Yogurt-Dill Sauce)

Raita *is an Indian condiment based on yogurt. It is not spicy at all, just very fresh and flavorful. I like to serve this with Medium-Rare Greek Meatloaf (page 92), Aloo Cholay (page 54), rice, or broccoli. You could also add some halved cherry tomatoes for a colorful, quick salad.*

HANDS-OFF: 15 MINUTES

SERVES 4 TO 6

1 1/2 cups plain yogurt

1/2 unpeeled cucumber (about 4 inches long)

1 tablespoon chopped fresh dill, or 1/2 teaspoon dried dill

1 teaspoon salt

1/2 teaspoon ground cumin

1. Put the yogurt in a medium nonreactive bowl. Halve the cucumber lengthwise and scoop out the seeds. On the large holes of a box grater, grate the cucumber into the bowl of yogurt. Add the dill, salt, and cumin and stir well to combine.

2. Refrigerate the sauce for at least 15 minutes for the flavors to combine. Serve cold.

Ceviche with Lime

When it's 105 degrees outside in summer, I have no interest in cooking something hot (unless it's grilled!). This seafood salad is a great way to have a light, refreshing meal that's not just a green salad. As with any ceviche, the lime juice "cooks" the tuna by altering the protein so that it's no longer raw, but without exposure to heat. You can use both cilantro leaves and stems by chopping them well. Do be sure to get fresh, high-quality tuna for the best flavor and texture.

HANDS-OFF: 30 MINUTES

SERVES 6 AS AN APPETIZER OR LIGHT MEAL

1 pound high-quality tuna
1/2 cup freshly squeezed lime juice
1/4 cup low-sodium soy sauce
1 tablespoon crushed ginger from a jar
1 teaspoon wasabi powder
1 teaspoon sugar
4 scallions, finely chopped, including green parts
1/4 cup chopped well-rinsed fresh cilantro
1 tablespoon black or white sesame seeds, toasted (see Note)
11/2 teaspoons toasted sesame oil

1. With a sharp knife, cut the tuna into small (1/2-inch square) pieces.

2. In a nonreactive bowl, whisk together the lime juice, soy sauce, ginger, wasabi, and sugar. Add the tuna, scallions, cilantro, sesame seeds, and oil. Stir to coat the tuna evenly.

3. Cover and refrigerate for at least 30 minutes for the flavors to come together. Serve within 2 days for the best texture.

Eye Appeal: Black sesame seeds add a great color contrast, but regular white seeds work just as well for flavor.

Note: To toast sesame seeds, put them in a dry skillet over medium-low heat and stir gently until they begin to smell fragrant, about 5 minutes. Remove them from the pan and set aside to cool.

Charleston Chicken-Pecan Salad

My cousin Dan got married in Charleston, South Carolina, and they served a delicious chicken-pecan salad with apples at the reception. It inspired me to make this recipe, which uses canned chicken, much like tuna salad. I usually like a chunkier chicken salad, with lots of roasted or grilled chicken. But the canned chicken and smoother consistency are more like the original in Charleston and make it easy to spread on bread for sandwiches; try Irish Soda Bread (page 153). This also makes a good hors d'oeuvre spread on crackers or bread rounds.

HANDS-OFF: 15 MINUTES

SERVES 6 AS A SANDWICH SPREAD

Three 5-ounce cans chicken breast meat without salt, drained, or about 10 ounces boneless, skinless chicken breasts

1/2 Granny Smith apple

1/2 cup (2 ounces) finely chopped pecans

1/2 cup Miracle Whip or similar salad dressing (zestier than mayonnaise)

2 scallions, thinly sliced, including 4 inches of green parts

2 teaspoons freshly squeezed lemon juice

1/4 teaspoon dry mustard

1. If using chicken breasts, poach them in simmering water for 12 to 15 minutes, or until just opaque throughout. Drain and cool briefly, then finely chop the meat in a food processor.

2. Using the large holes of a box grater, shred the unpeeled apple down to the core.

3. In a large bowl, combine the apple, chicken, pecans, dressing, scallions, lemon juice, and mustard. Mix well to break up the chicken and distribute the ingredients. Taste and adjust the seasoning.

4. Let stand for 15 minutes to allow the flavors to come together, or cover and refrigerate for up to 3 days. Spread on slices of bread and serve as sandwiches.

Shredded Carrot Salad

**HANDS-OFF:
15 MINUTES**

This is another recipe where the hands-off time is in the refrigerator. The flavors need time to mingle with each other and fully bloom. This colorful dish has a Middle Eastern flavor to it, with the lemony crushed coriander seeds, but it is refreshing as a side to virtually anything. You'll save yourself some elbow grease if you buy bags of shredded carrots in the refrigerated produce area. Serve this with Egyptian Macaroni en Crema (page 84), Garlic-Roasted Chicken with Orange (page 116), or as part of a salad buffet.

SERVES 4 TO 6

2 teaspoons coriander seeds

2 cups (about 8 ounces) shredded
 carrots

1/2 cup raisins

1/4 cup unsalted roasted sunflower
 seeds

2 tablespoons freshly squeezed
 lemon juice

2 tablespoons extra-virgin olive oil

Freshly ground black pepper to taste

1. Put the coriander seeds in a heavy plastic bag and use the bottom of a skillet or bowl to crack them. In a small, dry skillet, toast the coriander over low heat, undisturbed, until it is fragrant, about 5 minutes.

2. In a medium bowl, combine the carrots, raisins, sunflower seeds, lemon juice, oil, coriander, and a generous grinding of pepper. Stir everything well to distribute the ingredients.

3. Refrigerate for at least 15 minutes before serving, for the flavors to come together. Serve cold or at room temperature.

Pesto-Ricotta Soufflés

These mock soufflés were inspired by a side dish served at The Back Porch restaurant in Rehoboth, Delaware, where I used to work. They are tender inside, shot through with the green of the pesto, and browned on top. Serve these as a side to Quick Cranberry Turkey (page 138) or for a light meal with a green salad.

SERVES 6

1 teaspoon unsalted butter, melted

One 15-ounce tub low-fat ricotta cheese

3 large eggs

2 large egg whites

3 tablespoons prepared pesto

3 tablespoons all-purpose flour

1/2 teaspoon salt

1/4 teaspoon freshly ground black pepper

2 cups half-and-half

6 tablespoons (1 1/2 ounces) grated Parmesan cheese

Very hot water, as needed

1. Preheat the oven to 400°F. Coat the insides of six 8-ounce ramekins with the butter. Put them in a baking pan or casserole at least 2 inches deep and large enough to allow space between the ramekins.

2. In a large bowl, whisk together the ricotta, eggs, egg whites, pesto, flour, salt, and pepper until smooth. Gradually whisk in the half-and-half. Use a ladle to evenly fill the ramekins. Top each with a sprinkle of 1 tablespoon of the Parmesan.

3. Transfer the pan to the oven and carefully pour very hot water into the pan to come halfway up the sides of the ramekins. Bake for 40 to 45 minutes, or until the soufflés are risen, golden brown, and barely jiggly when moved.

4. Carefully remove the pan from the oven and let the soufflés sit in the hot water for 10 minutes to set. Use tongs to remove the ramekins from the water to a towel to dry, then serve immediately.

Hoppin' Bob

Hoppin' John is a classic South Carolina dish of rice and black-eyed peas. It's traditionally served on New Year's Day to ensure good luck in the coming year. To make this more substantial and colorful, I added corn and tomatoes. My husband likes to eat this with hot sauce, and I've named my version after him. Serve it as a side dish, under a stew, or with another South Carolina dish, Country Captain (page 118).

SERVES 8 TO 10

3 cups chicken or vegetable broth

One 15-ounce can black-eyed peas, drained and rinsed

One 14$1/2$-ounce can petite-cut tomatoes with jalapeños

1$1/2$ cups long-grain white rice

1 cup frozen corn kernels

1 teaspoon salt

Hot sauce, for serving

1. In a medium pot, stir together the broth, peas, tomatoes (with their juice), rice, corn, and salt. Cover the pot and set it over medium heat to cook until the rice is tender, about 30 minutes. Serve immediately, with plenty of hot sauce for garnish.

Chile-Corn Pudding

My mother served corn pudding throughout my childhood, and it's still a favorite recipe of my family's. I add roasted green chiles for both color and **HANDS-OFF: 30 MINUTES** a bit of extra flavor. Of course, you can always make it without them. You can use any kind of milk for this—from soy milk to whole milk to half-and-half. This is wonderful served with grilled meat and a simple tomato salad.

SERVES 4

2 tablespoons unsalted butter, melted

1 cup milk

2 large eggs

2 tablespoons sugar

2 tablespoons all-purpose flour

1 teaspoon baking powder

1/2 teaspoon salt

2 cups fresh or frozen corn kernels

1/2 cup (2 ounces) shredded Cheddar cheese (optional)

1/4 cup canned diced roasted green chiles (about half a 4-ounce can)

1. Preheat the oven to 350°F.

2. Pour the butter into a 9-inch casserole or pie plate.

3. In a medium bowl, whisk together the milk, eggs, sugar, flour, baking powder, and salt until combined and no lumps remain. Whisk in the corn, cheese (if using), and chiles.

4. Pour the mixture into the casserole and make sure the corn is well distributed, moving it around with a spoon if necessary. Bake for 30 minutes, or until the pudding is brown on top and set in the middle. Serve immediately.

Eye Appeal: If you don't like the heat of chiles, substitute chopped roasted red bell peppers. They'll be a nice color contrast to the yellow corn as well.

Cheesy Yummy Baked Polenta

**HANDS-OFF:
25 MINUTES**

I started out wanting to make baked grits—basically the same grind of corn as polenta—but they're pretty hard to find out in California. Coarsely ground corn is often labeled "polenta" if it's yellow and "grits" if it's white, but they are fairly interchangeable. So I made this with polenta, which is much more available. If you have grits, by all means use them here. I served this with the Ratatouille-Stuffed Baked Onions (page 94) for a taste-test dinner and they went together very well.

SERVES 8

1½ cups boiling or very hot water

1 cup uncooked polenta or grits

½ teaspoon salt

1 large egg

1½ cups milk

½ cup (2 ounces) shredded pepper
  jack cheese

½ teaspoon dried oregano

2 tablespoons unsalted butter,
  melted

1. Preheat the oven to 375°F.

2. In a medium bowl, pour the water over the polenta and salt and stir just to combine. Set aside.

3. In a large bowl, beat the egg. Whisk in the milk, cheese, and oregano. Add the polenta mixture to the bowl and whisk everything together well to remove any large lumps.

4. Pour the butter into a 10-inch pie plate or casserole. Pour the batter into the plate and bake for 25 to 30 minutes, or until the surface is puffed and a knife in the center comes out clean. Serve immediately.

Apple-Carrot Soufflé

**HANDS-OFF:
30 MINUTES**

This is a mock soufflé and similar to the Jewish dish tzimmes. It is a comforting warm purée that works well as a side dish at Thanksgiving or with Garlic-Roasted Chicken with Orange (page 116). The pecans add a welcome crunch to the otherwise smooth texture. If you have leftover cooked carrots, by all means use those instead of the canned. Make sure you have some crusty bread to dip in this at dinner.

SERVES 6

Two 14 1/2-ounce cans sliced carrots, drained, or 2 cups sliced carrots

2 cups applesauce

1 orange, zested and juiced

2 tablespoons unsalted butter, melted

1 tablespoon honey

2 tablespoons all-purpose flour

1 teaspoon ground cinnamon

1 teaspoon salt

1/4 teaspoon freshly ground black pepper

1/8 teaspoon ground cloves

1/8 teaspoon ground nutmeg

1/2 cup (2 ounces) chopped pecans or walnuts

1. Preheat the oven to 425°F. Lightly coat a 2-quart baking dish with oil or nonstick cooking spray.

2. If using fresh carrots, combine them in a dish with 2 tablespoons of water and microwave them on high for 5 minutes, or until tender. Or, on a stovetop in a sauté pan, simmer the carrots with about 1/2 cup water for 5 to 10 minutes, or until tender; drain.

3. In a food processor, process the carrots, applesauce, orange juice, and zest until smooth. Scrape the mixture into a large bowl and whisk in the butter, honey, flour, cinnamon, salt, pepper, cloves, and nutmeg until combined. Scrape the mixture into the baking dish and smooth the surface. Scatter the pecans on top.

4. Bake for 30 minutes, or until the nuts are toasted and the soufflé is heated through. Serve immediately, or cover and keep warm for 15 to 20 minutes. This soufflé will hold its heat well if kept covered.

Maple Sausage-Stuffed Apples

Here's a perfect fall appetizer or side dish. Use crisp and tart apples, like Gala or Granny Smith. Any type of bulk (uncooked) maple-flavored sausage would work well. The maple and apple make a wonderful sweet counterpoint to the savory sausage and sage. Serve this as a side to One-Pan Chicken (page 123) or as part of an apple-harvest meal with Apple-Cheddar Quiche (page 61) and Baked Beans with Apples and Jalapeño (page 28).

SERVES 6

1/3 cup (1 1/2 ounces) pine nuts or
   walnuts
6 large tart apples, such as Gala or
   Granny Smith
Ground cinnamon, for dusting
12 ounces maple-flavored bulk
   sausage
1 tablespoon minced fresh sage,
   or 1 teaspoon dried sage
1/2 teaspoon salt
1/3 cup apple cider or broth

1. Preheat the oven to 350°F.

2. Put the nuts in a baking dish and toast them in the oven for 10 minutes while preparing the apples.

3. Trim off about 1/2 inch from the top of each apple. Use the large end of a melon baller to scoop out the core and middle of each apple, leaving about 1/4 inch apple on the sides and bottom. Use the scoop to smooth the inside edges where possible. Set the apples in a 7 × 11–inch casserole or large baking dish so that there is some room between them. Dust the insides lightly with cinnamon.

4. In a medium bowl, mix together the sausage, nuts, sage, and salt until well combined. Divide the sausage among the apples, patting it into the cavities gently. Pour the cider around the apples in the casserole.

5. Bake for 50 minutes, or until the apples are tender and the sausage is cooked. Serve immediately.

Rosemary Yorkshire Pudding

This is a savory custard pudding traditionally made by putting the batter in a pan directly below roasting meat to catch the juices. Here, it is made with fresh rosemary to add a perfume to the dish. My mother always made this kind of recipe in a cast-iron muffin tin to form "popovers." If you want less of a crunch at the edges and a softer texture, bake this in a 9-inch square pan. It's a wonderful complement to Perfect Pot Roast (page 106) or Caramelized-Onion Brisket (page 85). I like just a bit of crunchy sea salt on top.

HANDS-OFF: 20 MINUTES

SERVES 6 TO 8

2 tablespoons unsalted butter or pan drippings

1 cup milk

1 cup all-purpose flour

3 large eggs

1 tablespoon minced fresh rosemary, or 1 teaspoon dried rosemary

1/2 teaspoon salt

Sea salt, for garnish (optional)

1. Preheat the oven to 400°F.

2. Put a 9 × 13–inch baking pan or casserole in the oven with the butter.

3. Meanwhile, in a large bowl, whisk together the milk, flour, eggs, rosemary, and salt until smooth. Turn down the oven to 375°F and pour the batter into the hot pan with the melted butter.

4. Bake for 20 to 25 minutes, or until the pudding is puffed and golden brown at the edges. Sprinkle on a bit of sea salt, if using, and serve immediately, cut into squares.

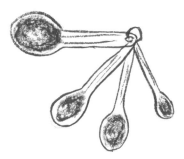

Baked Beans with Apples and Jalapeño

In Houston, there's a restaurant called Goode Company that we have to visit every time we're in town. They have great barbecue and baked beans, studded with chunks of apple and jalapeño. This is my take on that sweet and spicy side dish. It would be great served with Carolina Pulled Pork (page 108) and Mason-Dixon Cornbread (page 149).

SERVES 4 TO 6

1¹/2 cups apple cider or unfiltered
    apple juice
¹/4 cup ketchup
2 tablespoons molasses
Two 15-ounce cans white kidney
    beans, drained and rinsed
1¹/2 cups chopped firm apples,
    such as Granny Smith
¹/2 cup diced onion
1 large jalapeño chile, minced,
    or 2 tablespoons canned diced
    jalapeño
1 teaspoon dry mustard
¹/2 teaspoon salt
¹/2 teaspoon minced garlic
4 strips bacon, diced

1. Preheat the oven to 300°F.

2. In a large ovenproof pot or casserole, combine the cider, ketchup, molasses, beans, apples, onion, jalapeño, mustard, salt, and garlic. Stir well to combine. Scatter the bacon over the top.

3. Transfer the pot to the oven and bake, uncovered, until the apples are very soft and the liquid has reduced to a thick sauce, about 2 hours. Serve immediately.

Cranberry-Ginger Dressing

Whether you call this bread-based side dish dressing or stuffing may depend on where you grew up. It's part of a classic Thanksgiving meal, but consider serving it with meat or fish. The dried cranberries add a tart-sweet accent and some color. You could substitute another dried fruit if you prefer. This version is lighter and less dense than many recipes, so it's good as a side dish year-round.

SERVES 6 TO 8

1 pound crusty bread, such as
  walnut levain
2 cups diced onions
1 cup dried cranberries
1 cup diced celery
1/4 cup chopped candied (crystallized)
  ginger
1 tablespoon minced fresh thyme,
  or 1 teaspoon dried thyme
2 teaspoons minced garlic
1 orange, zested and juiced
1 teaspoon salt
1/4 teaspoon freshly ground black
  pepper
Chicken or vegetable broth,
  as needed
2 tablespoons olive oil

1. Preheat the oven to 375°F. Coat a 9 × 13–inch casserole with nonstick cooking spray.

2. Cut the bread into 1/2-inch dice and put it in a large bowl. Add the onions, cranberries, celery, ginger, thyme, garlic, orange zest, salt, and pepper. Measure the orange juice and add enough broth to equal 13/4 cups. Pour this mixture over the bread. Fold everything together thoroughly.

3. Press the dressing evenly into the casserole and drizzle the oil over the top.

4. Bake until the dressing is browned on top and heated through, about 45 minutes. Serve immediately.

soups & stews

Roasted Red Pepper Soup

HANDS-OFF:
30 MINUTES

What do you do with those jars of roasted red peppers? Try this easy soup, which is pretty as well, so it would be ideal for serving to guests. The addition of honey mellows the slight bitterness from the citric acid used to preserve the peppers.

SERVES 4

Two 12-ounce jars roasted red bell peppers, drained and rinsed

1 teaspoon olive oil

1/2 cup pico de gallo (see Note) or chunky salsa

2 cups chicken or vegetable broth

1 tablespoon honey

1 teaspoon minced garlic

1 teaspoon salt

Freshly ground black pepper, to taste

Chipotle hot sauce, to taste, for garnish (optional)

Crumbled goat cheese, for garnish (optional)

1. In a food processor or blender, purée the peppers.

2. In a medium saucepan, heat the oil over medium-high heat. Add the pico de gallo and stir once or twice. Add the puréed peppers, broth, honey, garlic, salt, and pepper. Set the lid ajar and turn the heat to low.

3. Simmer for 30 minutes, or until the soup is heated through and the flavors are combined. Taste and adjust the seasoning. If you like, garnish with hot sauce and goat cheese, which adds a creamy consistency when stirred into the soup. Additional pico de gallo would also be a nice garnish.

Note: Pico de gallo is often available in the refrigerated case of supermarkets. It contains chopped onion, tomato, and cilantro, and sometimes garlic and chiles. It's a great way to add quick flavor to dishes.

Gumbo Rapide

HANDS-OFF:
30 MINUTES

Gumbo is a great example of the New Orleans tradition of using local ingredients with a variety of immigrant influences. It embodies the diverse and unique character of a wonderful place. A classic gumbo calls for okra and gumbo filé, which is powdered sassafras leaves. Filé thickens gumbo slightly and adds a distinct flavor. So if you have a packet that you bought on a trip to New Orleans, make use of it now. My neighbor, Ari Branson, added tomatoes and yellow bell pepper when she tested this recipe and I really liked the results. Serve this over hot rice with extra hot sauce on the side.

SERVES 5 TO 6

1/4 cup vegetable oil

1/2 cup all-purpose flour

2 cups frozen sliced okra

One 14 1/2-ounce can diced tomatoes

1 cup diced yellow or red bell
   pepper

1 cup diced onion

1 cup thinly sliced celery

1 cup chopped fresh parsley

1 tablespoon minced garlic

1 pound 1/4-inch-thick ham steak
   or deli ham, cut into
   1/2-inch cubes

continues on next page

1. In a large pot over low heat, whisk together the oil and flour and let them cook while you chop the vegetables. This is a roux base. It may begin to get golden but should not turn brown.

2. In a large bowl, combine the okra, tomatoes, pepper, onion, celery, parsley, and garlic. Add the vegetables to the pot with the ham, shrimp, broth, hot sauce, vinegar, Worcestershire, and (if using) the gumbo filé. Stir to distribute everything well and set the pot lid ajar.

3. Cook until the vegetables are tender, about 30 minutes. Taste and add salt if needed. Serve immediately over rice with extra hot sauce.

12 to 16 ounces peeled raw
  medium shrimp
1 quart chicken or vegetable broth
2 tablespoons hot sauce
2 tablespoons red wine vinegar
1 tablespoon Worcestershire sauce
1 teaspoon gumbo filé (optional)
Salt, to taste (optional)

Hands-Off Technique: Most gumbo enthusiasts will tell you that a true gumbo needs a dark brown roux—a long-cooked fat and flour base—to give it the proper flavor. Since that's not very hands off, I've simplified the step a bit to allow for some cooking of the roux while you are doing other prep. If you happen to be a slow vegetable cutter, your roux will get darker, but don't ever let it burn. That just makes for bad gumbo.

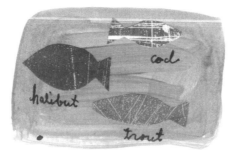

Lentil Soup with Greens and Sausage

**HANDS-OFF:
25 MINUTES**

When I subscribed to a weekly farm basket in San Francisco, we often got a lot of braising greens in the winter. This recipe was developed to help use some of those greens in a warming but quick soup. The carrots are al dente and sweet and add a nice color contrast. Look for bags of prewashed and chopped braising or Southern greens for this dish. I like to add a little olive oil if using a lower-fat poultry sausage, to help carry the flavors.

SERVES 4

8 ounces precooked Italian sausages

6 cups vegetable or chicken broth

1 tablespoon olive oil (optional)

1 cup lentils, rinsed

1 cup halved baby carrots

1 cup diced onion

1 teaspoon minced garlic

1 teaspoon salt

1 teaspoon dried thyme

1/4 teaspoon freshly ground black
   pepper

1 bay leaf

4 cups coarsely chopped braising
   greens, such as spinach, chard,
   and kale

1. Cut the sausage into 1/4-inch slices. In a large pot, combine the sausage with the broth, oil (if using), lentils, carrots, onion, garlic, salt, thyme, pepper, and bay leaf. Stir well to distribute the ingredients.

2. Set the pot lid ajar and turn the heat to medium-low. Simmer until the lentils are tender, about 25 minutes.

3. Put 1 cup of greens in each of 4 soup bowls. Top with 2 cups of the soup and serve immediately.

Hands-Off Technique: Putting the raw greens under the hot soup wilts them just enough without over-cooking them.

Eye Appeal: Add some diced red or yellow bell pepper for more color. Red or pink lentils make a nice color contrast to the greens.

Caribbean Black Bean Soup

HANDS-OFF:
40 MINUTES

Brothier than a classic black bean soup, this one is also colorfully studded with sweet potatoes and bell peppers. Ginger, coconut milk, allspice, and a touch of molasses give it an unmistakable Caribbean flavor. I made it first with a habanero (also known as Scotch bonnet) chile, but ended up liking the faint smokiness of chipotle better. Look for precut peeled sweet potatoes and crushed ginger in a jar to cut your prep time. You could also add 1 cup of shredded chicken or pork to this.

SERVES 6 TO 8

1 quart chicken or vegetable broth

One 15-ounce can lite coconut milk

1 medium sweet potato (about 1 pound), scrubbed and cut into 1/2-inch chunks

2 cups diced red onions

One 15-ounce can low-sodium black beans, drained and rinsed

1 cup diced yellow or red bell pepper

1/2 cup coarsely chopped fresh cilantro, divided

1 tablespoon molasses (not blackstrap)

2 teaspoons minced garlic

2 teaspoons crushed ginger from a jar

1 1/2 teaspoons salt

1 teaspoon chipotle hot sauce

1/2 teaspoon ground allspice

1. In a large pot, combine the broth, coconut milk, sweet potato, onions, beans, bell pepper, half of the cilantro, the molasses, garlic, ginger, salt, hot sauce, and allspice. Stir to distribute them well.

2. Set the pot over medium-low heat with the lid ajar. Simmer for 40 minutes, or until the sweet potato is tender and the soup is flavorful. Taste and adjust the seasoning. Serve garnished with the remaining cilantro.

Gingerrific Chicken Soup

**HANDS-OFF:
40 MINUTES**

I developed this recipe to help soothe a cold, but it's also good for easing the effects of allergies. Spicy ginger, combined with vitamin C–rich potatoes and lime, immune-boosting shiitake mushrooms, and vitamin A–packed carrots make this soup practically medicinal. Luckily, it's also delicious and lower in salt than canned soup—so don't limit it to days when you're sick. The soup freezes well, so you might as well make a big batch. However, if you want to halve it, cook it for just 30 minutes.

SERVES 6 TO 8

2 quarts chicken broth

About 1¼ pounds boneless, skinless chicken tenders

1 pound baby (new) red potatoes, cut into ½-inch chunks

2 cups baby carrots, cut into ½-inch chunks

4 ounces fresh shiitake mushrooms, stemmed and sliced, or 1 ounce dried shiitakes, rinsed and chopped

1 lime, zested and juiced

2-inch piece fresh ginger, peeled and thinly sliced

1 teaspoon salt

1 teaspoon freshly ground black pepper

1. Pour the broth into a large pot. Slice the chicken into bite-sized pieces and add to the broth along with the potatoes, carrots, mushrooms, lime zest and juice, ginger, salt, and pepper.

2. Set the pot over medium-low heat with the lid slightly ajar and simmer for 40 minutes, or until the chicken is cooked through and the potatoes are tender. Serve immediately or freeze and heat up as needed to soothe a cold.

Hands-Off Technique: To easily peel fresh ginger, use the edge of a spoon to scrape off just the papery skin.

Year-Round Corn Chowder

**HANDS-OFF:
35 MINUTES**

You don't need to wait for summer to enjoy this tasty chowder. Frozen corn is a great product to keep on hand. Of course, if you do have fresh corn, it will only improve the flavor of this easy soup. Buying prediced onions and bell pepper from the refrigerated section of the produce department will really decrease your prep time. Look for shelf-stable precooked bacon for this recipe as well.

SERVES 8

1/2 cup all-purpose flour

1 1/2 quarts chicken broth

1 cup half-and-half

3 cups (1 pound) frozen or fresh
   corn kernels

1 pound baby (new) red or yellow
   potatoes, quartered

1 cup diced onion

1 cup diced red bell pepper

1/4 cup diced cooked bacon

2 tablespoons unsalted butter

1 tablespoon sugar

1 teaspoon salt

1 teaspoon freshly ground black
   pepper

1 teaspoon dried thyme, or 1 tablespoon minced fresh thyme

1. In a large pot, whisk the flour into the broth until no lumps remain. Add the half-and-half, corn, potatoes, onion, bell pepper, bacon, butter, sugar, salt, pepper, and thyme and stir to combine.

2. Set the lid ajar and cook the chowder over medium-low heat for 35 minutes, or until the potatoes are tender. Serve immediately.

Panade (Bread Soup with Chard)

**HANDS-OFF:
1 HOUR**

The French word panade *can mean bread crumbs used as a thickening agent for a sauce, but in this case, it is a soup made with bread. This is a vegetarian version, but it has a hearty flavor from a long braising time in the oven. It's important to use a good crusty loaf of bread—preferably whole grain—and it's even better if the bread is a little stale. Buy it a day or two ahead and leave it unwrapped on the counter to dry out.*

SERVES 8 TO 10

10 to 12 ounces Swiss chard, thick stems trimmed

2 cups thinly sliced onions

1/2 ounce dried chanterelle mushrooms, rinsed

1 tablespoon minced garlic

1 teaspoon salt

1/2 teaspoon freshly ground black pepper

1/2 teaspoon dried thyme

1 loaf (about 1 pound) whole-grain pain au levain or other rustic bread, cut into 1/2-inch slices (you may not need all of them), stale or lightly toasted

continues on next page

1. Preheat the oven to 375°F.

2. Cut the chard across the leaves into 1-inch wide strips, discarding any large pieces of stem.

3. In a 5- to 7-quart Dutch oven or other heavy, deep casserole, layer half the onions, half the chard, and half the mushrooms. Sprinkle with the garlic, salt, pepper, and thyme. Top with a layer of bread, fitting it loosely. Add the remaining onions, chard, and mushrooms. Top with another layer of bread. In a small bowl, mix together the wine, oil, and honey to dissolve the honey. Pour over the top layer of bread. Pour on the broth. Scatter the cheese evenly over the top.

1/2 cup hearty dry red wine

2 tablespoons extra-virgin olive oil

1 tablespoon honey

2 quarts vegetable broth

1 cup (4 ounces) shredded Emmenthaler or Parmesan cheese

4. Cover the pot with aluminum foil (not the lid) and seal it around the edges. Cut 4 or 5 vents in the top. Set the pot on a rimmed baking sheet (jelly-roll pan) to catch any spillover. Bake for 1 hour, until the bread is very soft and the mushrooms are tender. Serve immediately, digging into the layers to get a bit of everything for each portion.

Gazpacho

This is what to make when it's too hot to cook and you have lots of tomatoes. I like to use Romas because they have fewer seeds, but any variety of ripe tomato will work. This is a bit more Italian in flavor than the classic Spanish version of gazpacho. Serve it with Spanish Omelette (page 65) or any crunchy salad.

SERVES 4 TO 6

2 pounds ripe tomatoes, cored
   and halved
1 cup packed fresh basil leaves,
   plus extra for garnish
1 large cucumber, peeled, seeded,
   and cut into chunks
1 red onion, quartered
1 teaspoon minced garlic
1/4 cup olive oil
2 tablespoons balsamic vinegar
1 teaspoon dried oregano
1 teaspoon salt
1/2 teaspoon freshly ground
   black pepper

1. In a food processor or blender, working in batches, pulse the tomatoes and 1 cup basil so that they are still chunky. Pour into a glass or ceramic bowl.

2. Add the cucumber, onion, garlic, oil, and vinegar to the food processor and pulse until the chunks are very small and evenly sized. Add them to the tomato mixture.

3. Add the oregano, salt, and pepper to the bowl and stir everything together well. Cover and refrigerate the gazpacho for at least 30 minutes for the flavors to come together. Before serving, taste and adjust the seasoning as needed. Garnish each portion with some fresh basil.

Chilled Avocado-Tomatillo Soup

HANDS-OFF: 20 MINUTES

Chilled avocado soup, you wonder? It's not just cold guacamole, but a smooth and refreshing dish with a gorgeous green color. There's a bit of spice to perk it up, and it's really eye-catching, with a dollop of plain yogurt and a few cherry tomato halves for garnish. It's also great served with some Mason-Dixon Cornbread (page 149). Look for canned tomatillos in the Mexican aisle of your grocery and hot or mild canned chiles, depending on your preference for spice.

SERVES 6

3 ripe avocados, halved, peeled, and pitted

One 11- or 12-ounce can tomatillos, drained

One 4-ounce can diced roasted green chiles

1/4 large red onion

1/4 cup freshly squeezed lime juice

1 tablespoon honey

1 teaspoon salt

1 teaspoon freshly ground black pepper

1/2 teaspoon ground coriander

2 cups vegetable broth

Plain yogurt or sour cream, for garnish

Halved cherry tomatoes, for garnish (optional)

1. In a food processor (or a blender, though it won't be as smooth), combine the avocado pulp, tomatillos, chiles, onion, lime juice, honey, salt, pepper, and coriander. Purée well, scraping down the sides at least once.

2. Pour the mixture into a large nonreactive bowl and whisk in the broth. Taste and adjust the seasoning. Cover and refrigerate the soup at least 20 minutes for the flavors to come together.

3. Serve the soup garnished with a dollop of yogurt and some tomatoes, if desired.

Eye Appeal: Chopped fresh cilantro, parsley, or even basil would be a lovely and fragrant garnish for this soup.

Pea Soup Ann

**HANDS-OFF:
1 HOUR**

I've always really liked split pea soup, but I didn't know until recently that it was Danish in origin. In California, if you drive down I-5, you see big billboards for the famous restaurant Pea Soup Andersen's. This is my version, with a bit of cardamom added for a distinct Scandinavian flavor. Sometimes you can find packaged diced prosciutto now; use that to save some prep time here and in other recipes. I add parsnip for a bit of sweet earthiness instead of carrots, which would change the bright green hue of this soup.

SERVES 6 TO 8

1 tablespoon unsalted butter

1 1/2 ounces prosciutto or
　bacon, diced (about 3 slices)

1 small parsnip

1 medium baby (new)
　red potato

1 pound dried split peas, rinsed

6 cups chicken broth

1 cup diced onion

1/2 teaspoon freshly ground white
　or black pepper

continues on next page

1. In a large pot over medium heat, combine the butter and prosciutto and leave to cook without stirring; the prosciutto will begin to crisp.

2. Meanwhile, shred the parsnip and potato by hand on the large holes of a box grater or in a food processor fitted with the grating disk. You should have about 1 cup each of the shredded parsnip and potato. Add the peas, parsnip, and potato to the pot with the prosciutto, then add the broth, onion, pepper, salt, and cardamom. Stir everything well to distribute the ingredients.

3. Reduce the heat to medium-low and set the pot lid ajar. Simmer for about 1 hour, or until the peas can be mashed

1/2 teaspoon salt

1/4 teaspoon ground cardamom

Rye cracker toasts, such as RyKrisp, for garnish (optional)

easily with a spoon. Use the back of a large spoon to mash some of the peas against the bottom of the pot. Serve the soup with rye crackers, if desired.

Hands-Off Technique: It's not very hands off, but if you prefer a fully puréed soup, use a hand-held immersion blender to purée the soup directly in the pot. It will only take a few minutes.

Red Beans and Andouille

Dried beans are ideal for a slow cooker because they can be left for hours to cook while you work or do other things! They're also less expensive than canned beans and don't have the added sodium. This dish can be hot or mild, depending on the type of sausage and peppers that you choose. Andouille sausage is a spicy sausage frequently used in Cajun cooking. Though not authentic, other types of smoked sausage such as kielbasa work equally well here. This stew is great alone or over rice or Mason-Dixon Cornbread (page 149).

SERVES 6 TO 8

1 1/2 quarts chicken or vegetable broth

1 tablespoon olive oil

1 pound dried pinto or kidney beans, rinsed

1 pound andouille or other cured sausage, sliced 1/2 inch thick

1 cup diced onion

1 red Anaheim or bell pepper, diced

1/2 cup sliced baby carrots

2 teaspoons minced garlic

Salt, to taste

1. In a slow cooker, combine the broth, oil, beans, sausage, onion, pepper, carrots, and garlic. Stir and cover.

2. Set the cooker on low and cook for 7 to 8 hours, or until the beans are tender. Stir in salt, if needed. (Don't do this at the beginning, or the beans may not soften adequately.) Mash some of the beans against the side of the pot to thicken the stew, if desired. Serve immediately.

Eye Appeal: Choose a green or yellow pepper rather than red, because it gives a better color contrast to the red beans and sausage.

Brunswick Stew

HANDS-OFF: 8 HOURS

Brunswick stew is a mid-Atlantic and Southern favorite, classically made with squirrel! This was always one of my favorite meals growing up, and I even resorted to heating up canned Brunswick stew in an electric hot pot when I went to college. Serve this with Irish Soda Bread (page 153) or Mason-Dixon Cornbread (page 149) and a green salad.

SERVES 8 TO 10

1 tablespoon vegetable oil

1/2 cup all-purpose flour

1/2 teaspoon salt

1/2 teaspoon freshly ground black pepper, plus more to taste

About 3 pounds boneless, skinless chicken thighs and breasts

1 1/2 cups (9 ounces) dried baby lima beans, rinsed

1 pound baby (new) potatoes, halved

One 14 1/2-ounce can diced tomatoes

1 1/2 cups (8 ounces) frozen or canned and drained corn kernels

1 cup diced onion

1 teaspoon dried thyme

1 bay leaf

2 1/2 cups chicken broth

1. Turn on a slow cooker to low and add the oil.

2. Combine the flour, salt, and pepper in a shallow dish or plastic bag. Toss the chicken pieces in the flour and add them to the cooker. Add the beans to the cooker next, followed by the potatoes, tomatoes, corn, onion, thyme, and bay leaf, adding the broth last.

3. Cover the pot and cook for about 8 hours, or until the beans are tender; this can cook a bit longer if necessary. You want the chicken to fall apart. Serve immediately, with freshly ground pepper on top.

Pork Chili with Sweet Potatoes

HANDS-OFF:
45 MINUTES

This is not a tomato-based chili, but a chile pepper–based stew inspired by the Texas style of chilis. And since I can't possibly compete with my native-Texan husband in making Texas chili, I've used pork, sweet potatoes, and beans—all out of the question for classic Lone Star chili. But the milder flavor of pork, slightly sweetened by the potatoes and the "secret" ingredient, maple syrup, is a nice substitute.

My theory of making chili is that you might as well make a big batch—so this feeds 6 to 8 hungry cowpokes and freezes very well for future meals. Make sure not to buy chili powder but ground pure chiles, available in the spice aisle or Mexican foods department of grocery stores. Serve this with Mason-Dixon Cornbread (page 149).

If possible, ask your butcher to give you "chili grind" for the ground pork.

SERVES 6 TO 8

2 tablespoons olive oil

2 cups diced onions

1 1/2 pounds coarsely ground pork
(such as shoulder)

1 1/2 pounds unpeeled long, thin
garnet yams or sweet potatoes

5 1/2 cups chicken broth

1/2 cup bourbon or additional
chicken broth

2 tablespoons maple syrup

continues on next page

1. In a large pot, heat the oil over medium-high heat until shimmering. Add the onions and pork, stirring just to break up the meat, and leave to brown.

2. Meanwhile, trim and cut the yams into quarters lengthwise, then into 1/4-inch slices crosswise. Add the yams to the pot, followed by the broth, bourbon, syrup, beans, chile, garlic, oregano, salt, cinnamon, and cumin. Stir well to combine everything.

3. Turn the heat to medium-low and set the pot lid ajar. Simmer for about 45 minutes, or until the pork and

Two 14½-ounce cans black beans,
    drained and rinsed
¾ cup (about 3¼ ounces) ground
    pure chile, such as ancho or New
    Mexico
2 teaspoons minced garlic
1 teaspoon dried oregano
1 teaspoon salt
1 teaspoon ground cinnamon
½ teaspoon ground cumin
Sour cream, shredded cheese, and
    minced fresh cilantro, for garnish
    (optional)

potatoes are tender. Serve the chili immediately, with sour cream, shredded cheese, and cilantro alongside to garnish, if you like.

Hands-Off Technique: Chili recipes traditionally call for sautéeing the meat and onions first. Here, they are left to brown without stirring while you complete the other ingredient prep. You get a similar effect without having to attend the pot.

Beef and Barley Stew

Usually you see red wine added to beef stew, à la beef bourguignonne. I found an old recipe from Julia Child using beer, though, and then I remembered that beer is made with barley. So this stew is a hearty mixture of beef, barley, and amber beer. A darker beer would be too bitter, so stick to a "red" or amber ale. Serve this with some crusty warm bread for sopping up the sauce.

SERVES 4 TO 6

2 pounds precut beef chuck or
   stew meat

Salt

Freshly ground black pepper

One 10-ounce package frozen pearl
   onions or fresh pearl onions, peeled

1 cup diced bell pepper

1/2 ounce dried sliced portobello
   mushrooms, rinsed

1 tablespoon minced garlic

1 cup pearl barley, rinsed

continues on next page

1. Set a large pot over medium-high heat. If the beef cubes are large, cut them into 3/4-inch pieces. Season the beef with salt and pepper. To the heated pot, add the beef, onions, bell pepper, mushrooms, garlic, barley, sugar, thyme, and bay leaf. Add 1 teaspoon salt and 1/4 teaspoon pepper. Add the broth and beer. Stir everything well to distribute the ingredients.

2. Reduce the heat to low and cover the pot. Simmer for 1 hour and 15 minutes, or until the beef and barley are both tender. Serve immediately.

2 tablespoons packed light brown
   sugar
1 teaspoon dried thyme
1 bay leaf
2 cups beef broth
One 12-ounce bottle amber or
   "red" beer

Hands-Off Technique: Most stews call for sautéeing the meat before adding the other ingredients. That's not very hands off though, so here the beef is added to a hot pot so it browns slightly while you're adding the other ingredients.

Eye Appeal: This stew is delicious, but rather brown, so add some diced red bell pepper, carrot coins, or minced fresh parsley for a hit of color.

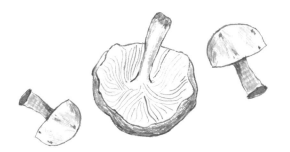

Spinach Dal

This vegetarian dish is based on one I learned from copyediting the book Nepali Home Cooking by Jyoti Pathak. It's delicious served with rice to soak up the juices, and I almost always seem to have the ingredients on hand for a last-minute dinner if I'm otherwise uninspired. Make sure not to use creamed spinach. The frozen chopped variety works beautifully. Serve this with warm naan or tortillas and the Indian-style Chicken with Raisins and Almonds (page 132).

SERVES 4 TO 6

3 cups water

3 tablespoons unsalted butter

1 cup red or pink lentils, rinsed

3 cups frozen chopped spinach or
   chard (not creamed) or 4 cups
   fresh spinach or chard

One 14 1/2-ounce can diced tomatoes

1/2 cup diced onion

2 teaspoons minced garlic

1 1/2 teaspoons crushed ginger
   from a jar

1 teaspoon ground cumin

1 teaspoon salt

1. In a large pot, combine the water, butter, lentils, spinach, tomatoes, onion, garlic, ginger, cumin, and salt and stir well to mix the ingredients.

2. Set the pot over medium-low heat and simmer, uncovered, for 25 minutes, or until the lentils are tender. Serve immediately, or cover and keep warm for up to 30 minutes.

Lamb Tagine

Tagine is a Moroccan stew named for the pot in which it's traditionally cooked, and the many varieties of this dish are characterized by a sweet and sour flavor. A tagine pot has a conical lid, to help hold steam, but you can use a regular pot with a tight-fitting lid. Look for lamb stew meat or have your butcher cube a boneless shoulder or leg. This is wonderful over hot rice or couscous. Look for chopped dates to cut your prep time a bit.

SERVES 4

1 tablespoon olive oil

2 pounds cubed lamb

Salt

Freshly ground black pepper

One 15-ounce can chickpeas, drained and rinsed

One 10-ounce bag frozen pearl onions or fresh pearl onions, peeled

1 cup chopped dates

1 cup packed coarsely chopped fresh cilantro

1/2 cup coarsely chopped fresh mint, divided

1 orange, zested and juiced

1 tablespoon red wine vinegar

1/2 teaspoon ground cinnamon

Large pinch of saffron

1 cup water

1. In a large pot, heat the oil over medium-high heat until shimmering. Sprinkle the lamb with salt and pepper, add to the pot in a single layer, and leave it to brown.

2. Meanwhile, combine the chickpeas, onions, dates, cilantro, half of the mint, the orange zest, 1 teaspoon salt, the vinegar, cinnamon, and saffron in a bowl. Pour them on top of the lamb. Pour in the orange juice and water and stir to combine everything well.

3. Reduce the heat to medium-low and cover the pot. Simmer for about 1 hour, or until the lamb is very tender. Serve immediately, over rice or couscous, garnished with the remaining mint.

Aloo Cholay (Chickpea-Potato Curry)

This is my take on a classic Indian mild chickpea-potato curry. I usually serve it with basmati rice and naan, tortillas, or pitas. When Indian cooks call for "chili powder," they usually mean cayenne, which I use here. If you like your food a little less spicy, use a Southwestern chili powder to add some flavor but not much spice. This is great with a dollop of Raita (page 17).

SERVES 4 TO 6

2½ cups vegetable broth or water

Two 15-ounce cans chickpeas, drained and rinsed

One 14½-ounce can fire-roasted or stewed tomatoes with chiles

6 baby (new) Yukon Gold potatoes (about 12 ounces), quartered

1 cup diced onion

1 tablespoon unsalted butter

2 teaspoons crushed ginger from a jar

2 teaspoons salt

1 teaspoon ground cumin

1 teaspoon ground coriander

½ teaspoon cayenne pepper

1. In a large pot, combine the broth, chickpeas, tomatoes, potatoes, onion, butter, ginger, salt, cumin, coriander, and cayenne. Stir to mix and nestle the potatoes into the liquid.

2. Set the pot, uncovered, over medium heat. Simmer vigorously for about 35 minutes, or until the potatoes are tender. Serve the curry in bowls with Indian naan bread or over rice.

Smoky Manhattan Clam Chowder

*I*f you're not familiar with chowder lingo, "Manhattan" indicates the use of to-matoes vs. milk or cream in this hearty soup. To make the flavor more complex, I've added smoked whole baby clams, a really flavorful product that is readily available. You can use fresh shucked clams or canned for the remainder, although canned are probably more traditional for many home cooks. Serve this with some crusty bread and a salad.

SERVES 8 TO 10

4 slices bacon, diced

1 cup diced onion

4 medium baby (new) potatoes

3 stalks celery

1 quart chicken broth

One 14$\frac{1}{2}$-ounce can crushed
   tomatoes

One 14$\frac{1}{2}$-ounce can petite-cut
   tomatoes

One 4-ounce can baby clams, or
   10 ounces fresh clams, shucked

Two 3-ounce tins smoked baby
   clams, drained

1$\frac{1}{2}$ teaspoons minced garlic

1 teaspoon dried oregano

1. Set a large pot over medium-high heat and add the bacon and onion. Stir once or twice and leave it to sizzle.

2. Meanwhile, cut the potatoes into 6 or 8 pieces each and dice the celery. Add them to the pot with the broth, both kinds of tomatoes, both kinds of clams, the garlic, and oregano and stir well.

3. Set the pot lid ajar and turn the heat to medium-low. Simmer until the potatoes are tender, about 40 minutes. Taste and adjust the seasoning as desired before serving.

Hands-Off Technique: Putting the bacon and the onion in a preheated pot lets them soften and brown slightly while you finish preparing the rest of the ingredients. Open all of the cans before you begin adding everything on top of the bacon and onion.

savory pies & tarts

Fridge-Cleaning Frittata

This is a great recipe for using up the odds and ends of vegetables, meat, and cheese in your fridge. It works well with just about any vegetable—raw or cooked. However, if you want to use potatoes, either cut them in 1/2-inch dice or use precooked chunks. Any meat you add should be precooked; just cut it into bite-sized pieces. Serve this for brunch or a light dinner with a green salad.

HANDS-OFF: 25 MINUTES

SERVES 4 TO 6

1 tablespoon unsalted butter or oil

8 large eggs

1/2 cup milk

1 teaspoon salt

1/2 teaspoon freshly ground black pepper

1 cup (4 ounces) grated Parmesan cheese, divided

1 cup vegetable pieces, such as broccoli or zucchini (or use some precooked meat)

3 scallions, including green parts, thinly sliced

1/4 cup oil-packed slivered sun-dried tomatoes, drained

1/2 teaspoon minced garlic

1. Preheat the oven to 350°F.

2. Put the butter in a 9- to 10-inch ovenproof skillet (such as cast iron) and put the skillet in the oven for at least 2 minutes for the butter to melt.

3. Meanwhile, in a medium bowl, whisk together the eggs, milk, salt, and pepper until combined and frothy. Stir in 3/4 cup of the cheese, along with the vegetables, scallions, tomatoes, and garlic.

4. Remove the skillet from the oven. Pour the egg mixture into the skillet. Sprinkle the remaining 1/4 cup cheese over the top. Bake the frittata for 25 to 30 minutes, or until the top puffs and is lightly browned. Serve immediately or cool completely, wrap, and refrigerate (I've been known to eat cold leftovers for breakfast!).

Eye Appeal: Including some red vegetables, like peppers or tomatoes, adds great color to the frittata.

Tamale Pie

Tamale pie is a Texas tradition that I only learned about when I married a Texan. But I was already a fan of tamales, especially nacatamales, *the Nicaraguan version, with olives, roasted peppers, and prunes. This incorporates those flavors and the Texas idea of baking the casserole with a topping of cornbread. You can use a packaged cornbread mix or substitute a batch of Mason-Dixon Cornbread batter (page 149).*

SERVES 6 TO 8

1½ to 2 pounds ground chicken or
   turkey

½ cup pimiento-stuffed olives,
   drained and coarsely chopped

½ cup diced onion

½ cup packed chopped fresh parsley
   leaves

One 4-ounce can roasted diced green
   chiles, drained

¼ cup chopped prunes or raisins

1½ teaspoons chili powder

1 teaspoon ground cumin

½ teaspoon salt

½ cup chicken broth

One 1-pound box cornbread mix, or
   1 recipe Mason-Dixon Cornbread
   batter (page 149)

Milk, as needed

1. Preheat the oven to 350°F. Spray a 9 × 12–inch casserole with nonstick cooking spray.

2. In a large bowl, combine the chicken, olives, onion, parsley, chiles, prunes, chili powder, cumin, and salt. Use a spoon or spatula to break up the meat and distribute the ingredients without mashing the meat—you want chunks. Spoon the mixture into the casserole, patting it down slightly. Pour the broth on top.

3. In a medium bowl, prepare the cornbread according to the package directions, adding enough milk to make it pourable. Pour the cornbread batter over the meat and spread it as evenly as possible. It doesn't have to reach all the edges.

4. Bake the pie for 35 minutes, or until the top is browned and the meat is bubbling and cooked through. Let it sit for 15 minutes before serving, to allow the filling to set.

Apple-Cheddar Quiche

I love soufflés, and one of my favorite recipes is in the classic cookbook *The Enchanted Broccoli Forest* by Mollie Katzen. However, soufflés are sometimes intimidating, so I developed this quiche version. You can certainly make your own crust, but the frozen deep-dish crusts in most grocery stores work very well for this. I've also made the recipe with soy milk and it was just as good.

HANDS-OFF: 1 HOUR

SERVES 4 TO 6

1 large tart apple, such as Granny Smith
3 large eggs
1 cup milk
1/2 teaspoon salt
1/4 teaspoon ground cinnamon
1 cup (4 ounces) packed shredded sharp Cheddar cheese, divided
One frozen 9-inch deep-dish pie crust

1. Preheat the oven to 400°F.

2. On the large holes of a box grater, shred the apple, skin and all, stopping short of the core on each side.

3. In a large bowl, whisk together the eggs, milk, salt, and cinnamon. Stir in the shredded apple and 3/4 cup of the cheese. Pour the mixture into the crust and top it with the remaining 1/4 cup of cheese.

4. Bake the quiche for 30 minutes, or until it is puffed and golden. The center will still be a little wobbly. Remove the quiche to a wire rack or trivet and let it sit for 30 minutes to set before you cut it. Serve warm, or refrigerate and eat cold for a refreshing lunch or breakfast treat!

Jamaican Meat Pie

HANDS-OFF:
1 HOUR
20 MINUTES

Jamaican food has many culinary influences from Africa, including okra, peanuts, and ackee—a kind of fruit. Jamaicans are also well known for their jerk
seasoning, a combination of spices such as thyme, allspice, and Scotch bonnet chiles.
This recipe takes the classic hand-held Jamaican meat patty and makes it larger for an entrée dish.
A crunchy cornmeal and coconut crust offsets the savory, spiced meat. If you can't find unsweetened
coconut, either leave it out of the recipe or buy sweetened coconut and rinse it well to remove some of
the sugar. Serve this with a side of Banana Bread (page 154) for the full Caribbean experience.

SERVES 8

1 1/2 cups yellow or white cornmeal

1/2 cup unsweetened shredded
    coconut

1/2 cup water

1/4 cup vegetable oil

1 teaspoon dried thyme

1/2 teaspoon salt

One 8-ounce jar Jamaican jerk
    sauce

1 1/4 pounds ground turkey

1 cup frozen sliced okra

continues on next page

1. Preheat the oven to 425°F. Spray a 10-inch deep-dish
pie plate or 9-inch square baking dish with nonstick cooking spray.

2. In a medium bowl, mix together the cornmeal, coconut, water, oil, thyme, and salt until they are well combined. Pour the mixture into the pie plate and pat it up
the sides and over the bottom to make a fairly even crust.
Be careful not to let it build up too much in the crease of
the pan; the top edge can be uneven. Refrigerate the crust
while you prepare the filling.

1/2 cup diced onion

1/2 cup frozen peas and carrots

2 tablespoons white vinegar

1/4 teaspoon cayenne pepper (optional)

1/2 cup dried bread crumbs

3. First, taste the jerk sauce and see if it's spicy enough for you. If not, add the optional cayenne with the turkey. In a large bowl, combine the jerk sauce, turkey, okra, onion, peas and carrots, vinegar, and cayenne (if using). Use a spoon or spatula to break up the meat and distribute the ingredients without mashing the meat. Spread the turkey mixture in the crust, patting it down and mounding it slightly in the middle. Scatter the bread crumbs evenly over the top.

4. Bake the pie for 1 hour and 10 minutes, or until the crust is well browned and an instant-read thermometer reads 160°F when inserted in the center. Remove the pie and let it cool for 10 to 15 minutes before slicing it into wedges.

Gardener's Pie

**HANDS-OFF:
45 MINUTES**

*L*ike a shepherd's pie, this vegetarian casserole is topped with potatoes, but here they are shredded or "hash brown" potatoes, available in the refrigerated produce case of many groceries. A carrot adds some welcome color to the topping. If you don't like eggplant for the filling, then use other vegetables. You'll need about 6 cups total, not including the onion. Mushrooms, zucchini, and carrots would all be good substitutes. Serve this with Gazpacho (page 42) if your garden runneth over!

SERVES 8

1 cup vegetable broth

2 tablespoons low-sodium soy sauce

1 medium globe eggplant (about 12 ounces), cut into 3/4-inch cubes

1 cup frozen peas

1 cup diced onion

1/4 cup yellow or white cornmeal

1/2 cup (2 ounces) shredded fontina or Italian-blend cheeses

1/4 cup tomato paste

1 teaspoon minced garlic

1 teaspoon dried thyme

2 tablespoons olive oil

One 18-ounce bag shredded potatoes

1 large carrot, shredded

1/2 teaspoon salt

Freshly ground black pepper, to taste

1. Preheat the oven to 400°F. Spray a 9 × 12–inch casserole with nonstick cooking spray.

2. In a medium bowl, combine the broth, soy sauce, eggplant, peas, onion, cornmeal, cheese, tomato paste, garlic, and thyme. Mix well to distribute the paste and spices. Spread the mixture evenly in the casserole and pat it down slightly. In the same bowl, combine the oil, potatoes, carrot, and salt and mix well. Spread them evenly over the vegetables and pat them down. Grind pepper generously over the top.

3. Bake the pie for 40 minutes, or until the filling is bubbling and the potatoes are well browned and crispy. Let the casserole cool for 5 to 10 minutes before cutting it into portions.

Spanish Omelette

**HANDS-OFF:
40 MINUTES**

In Spain, this is a very popular tapa, *or snack with drinks. When I visited Ma-drid, though, I liked to order it for lunch. Called* tortilla española, *it is like a quiche in that there is no crust, but it does have lots of potatoes. This is classically served with a garlicky mayonnaise called* aioli, *but you can use regular mayonnaise or try it with Romesco Sauce (page 89) and serve a green salad on the side.*

SERVES 4 TO 6

12 ounces small waxy potatoes, such as baby (new) red

2 tablespoons olive oil

1/2 cup diced onion

1/2 cup chopped fresh parsley

5 large eggs

1 teaspoon baking powder

1 teaspoon salt

1/4 teaspoon freshly ground black pepper

Mayonnaise or Romesco Sauce (page 89), for garnish (optional)

1. Preheat the oven to 375°F.

2. Slice the potatoes very thinly on a mandoline or with a knife or box grater. Toss the potatoes with the oil in a 9-inch pie plate or casserole, then add the onion and parsley and toss again. Form the potatoes into a fairly even layer in the dish.

3. In a small bowl, beat together the eggs, baking powder, salt, and pepper until frothy. Pour over the potatoes and smooth the top. The potatoes will rise above the liquid, but that's okay.

4. Bake for 40 minutes, or until the potatoes are tender when pierced with a knife and the edges are brown. Slice the omelette into wedges or in squares for tapas. Serve each portion with mayonnaise or romesco sauce on the side.

Hands-Off Technique: A mandoline is a stand slicer that is readily available to home cooks now. You can find small, inexpensive plastic models (with metal blades) in Japanese groceries and larger models in stores like Target. They slice and shred very efficiently. Just make sure to use the hand guard.

Chicken Potpie

HANDS-OFF:
1 HOUR
10 MINUTES

Unless *you buy frozen potpies, you probably don't get a chicken potpie very of-ten. They're a cinch to make though, and much healthier if you make them from scratch. Plus, you get to use up extra bits of vegetables if you need to; prepare 5 cups in addition to the shallots. This version is topped with refrigerated pie dough (not the frozen preformed shells), a very good product widely available in supermarkets. Its crunch is a perfect counterpoint to the creamy thyme-scented sauce. Serve this with a simple salad or a first course of Roasted Red Pepper Soup (page 33) if it's cold and blustery outside.*

SERVES 4

1 (11-ounce) refrigerated pie crust

1 cup beef or chicken broth

1 cup buttermilk

1/2 cup all-purpose flour

1 pound chicken tenders, cut into
   1-inch pieces

21/2 cups (8 ounces) sliced mushrooms

1 cup frozen cut green and yellow
   Italian beans

1 cup 1/2-inch dice potatoes

continues on next page

1. Preheat the oven to 350°F. Spray a 2-quart casserole with nonstick cooking spray.

2. If you're using a round casserole, cut the pastry so that it's 1/2 inch wider than the casserole. If you're using a rectangular casserole, cut the pastry so that the pieces will fit on top. Put the pastry and any scraps back in the refrigerator to keep cold.

3. In a large bowl, whisk together the broth, buttermilk, and flour until smooth. Add the chicken, mushrooms, beans, potatoes, carrots, shallots, garlic, thyme, salt, and pepper. Mix well to distribute the sauce and spices. Spoon the mixture into the casserole.

1 cup frozen carrot coins

1/2 cup thinly sliced shallots or
diced onion

1 tablespoon minced garlic

1 teaspoon dried thyme

1 1/2 teaspoons salt

1/2 teaspoon freshly ground black
pepper

1 large egg

4. In a small bowl, whisk the egg to blend it. Bring out the pastry and brush the egg generously over one side of it. Flip it over and set it, egg side down, on top of the casserole. If there are any scraps, set them on top, if you want, and then lightly brush the whole top surface with egg. Cut 4 or 5 small vent holes with a sharp knife.

5. Bake the potpie on a rimmed baking sheet (jelly-roll pan) for 1 hour, or until the pastry is golden and puffed. Let it cool for 10 minutes before spooning out portions of filling and crust.

Stress Saver: Brushing the pastry with egg before topping the pie gives it a waterproofing. This should keep it from getting soggy while the filling simmers underneath. The top coating of egg also helps the pastry to brown attractively.

Sausage Strata

A strata is a layered savory bread pudding, hence the name, which means "layers" in Latin. Here, you use sliced bread layered with sausage, sun-dried tomatoes, and cheese, held together with a sage-scented custard. My mother sometimes serves a similar dish on Christmas morning because she can assemble it the night before and leave it in the fridge overnight. If you want to do that with this recipe, plan to bake it for about 5 minutes longer. Look for the new moist sun-dried tomatoes available in bags already julienned.

SERVES 6 TO 8

1 tablespoon olive oil

4 to 5 large slices sourdough or
   hearty white bread

2 sweet Italian sausages, casings
   removed

1/2 cup julienned sun-dried tomatoes

1 cup (4 ounces) shredded Gruyère
   cheese

3 cups milk

5 large eggs

1/2 teaspoon dried sage

1/4 teaspoon salt

1/4 teaspoon freshly ground black
   pepper

1. Preheat the oven to 375°F. Rub the bottom of a 2-quart casserole dish with the olive oil.

2. Make 1 layer of bread in the casserole dish, cutting the pieces to fit. Top the bread with crumbled bits of 1 sausage, then the tomatoes and half of the cheese. Repeat the layering with the remaining bread, sausage, and cheese.

3. In a medium bowl, whisk together the milk, eggs, sage, salt, and pepper. Pour the liquid evenly over the casserole. (At this point, you can cover it well and refrigerate it for up to 2 days until needed.)

4. Bake the strata for 45 minutes, until the top is browned and the custard is set. Let it rest for 10 to 15 minutes before cutting into squares.

Greek Leek and Greens Pie

HANDS-OFF:
45 MINUTES

We hear again and again how good dark, leafy greens are for us. But unless you're a Southerner, you probably don't eat a lot of them. Here's a wonderful recipe using frozen greens that don't get squishy and have plenty of flavor. It's based on a traditional Greek recipe that uses phyllo. I've used frozen puff pastry instead, which is much easier to handle. Just make sure to thaw it for at least 4 hours in the refrigerator before you need it. You can assemble this ahead of time and keep it covered and refrigerated for a day or two until you want to bake it. I served it as part of a Mediterranean dinner one night with Gazpacho (page 42).

SERVES 6

1 pound frozen chopped greens, such as spinach or collards (not creamed)

1²/3 cups (8 ounces) crumbled feta cheese

1 large leek, halved, well rinsed, and thinly sliced

1 cup diced onion

1 cup chopped fresh parsley

1/2 cup currants or raisins

1 tablespoon fennel seed

1/2 teaspoon salt

1/4 teaspoon freshly ground black pepper

1 sheet frozen puff pastry (from a 17.3-ounce box), thawed in the refrigerator

1. Preheat the oven to 375°F.

2. In a large bowl, mix together the greens, feta, leek, onion, parsley, currants, fennel seed, salt, and pepper. Spoon them into a 9 × 12–inch casserole and smooth the top.

3. Unfold the pastry and cut it along the fold lines. Stretch the strips slightly lengthwise to fit the pan and then lay them on top of the greens, overlapping them slightly.

4. Bake the pie for 45 minutes, or until the pastry is puffed and brown. Follow the lines of the pastry to cut the pie into 6 pieces and serve immediately.

Eye Appeal: Before putting it in the oven, brush the top of the pastry with a lightly beaten egg to add color and gloss to the surface.

Chicken-Pear Calzones

Calzones are essentially a larger version of empanadas, which are little meat pies made all over South America and the Caribbean. You'll often find them made there with beef and onions, olives, or peppers. The Argentineans like to add fruit like pears and peaches, though, and I like the idea of a fruit and poultry combination. These are a nice change from the typical tomato sauce and cheese filling of most calzones. The Asian pear adds extra crunchiness, but a regular firm pear works well too.

SERVES 2 TO 4

12 ounces ground chicken or turkey

1 small Asian or other firm pear, cored and diced

1/2 cup diced onion

1/2 cup diced bell pepper

1/4 cup chopped fresh cilantro

2 tablespoons olive oil, plus extra for garnish

1 tablespoon freshly squeezed lime juice

1 teaspoon minced garlic

1/2 teaspoon salt

continues on next page

1. Preheat the oven to 400°F with a pizza stone inside if you have one. Line a baking sheet with parchment paper.

2. In a medium bowl, combine the chicken, pear, onion, bell pepper, cilantro, the 2 tablespoons oil, the juice, garlic, salt, and pepper. Mix well to distribute the ingredients, but don't squash the meat.

3. On a well-floured work surface, cut the dough into 2 equal pieces. Roll each piece into a round about 8 inches in diameter. Place half of the meat mixture on one half of each round, leaving a 3/4-inch margin at the edge. Dab the edge with water, then fold over the round and press the edges together. Fold the edges back on top of themselves and press firmly again. Put the calzones on the prepared pan. Cut 2

1/4 teaspoon freshly ground black pepper

All-purpose flour, for kneading

1 pound refrigerated or frozen, thawed pizza dough

slits in the top of each calzone. Transfer the pan to the oven, or slide the calzones onto the preheated pizza stone.

4. Bake for 25 to 30 minutes, or until the calzones are golden brown. Drizzle with more olive oil before serving.

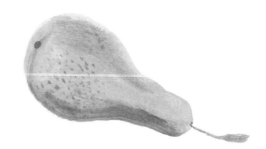

Savory Asparagus Bread Pudding

What is Thanksgiving dressing but a savory bread pudding? In fact, it's a perfect way to use leftover slightly stale bread or at least try a new side dish. *If you don't have leftover bread, try to buy a loaf one or two days ahead and let it sit on the counter to stale slightly. The asparagus here is a bright, flavorful addition, but you could certainly use other vegetables. Serve this with Garlic-Roasted Chicken with Orange (page 116) or as part of a spring vegetarian dinner with Chilled Avocado-Tomatillo Soup (page 43).*

HANDS-OFF: 55 MINUTES

SERVES 6 TO 8

One 1-pound loaf sourdough or other crusty bread

3 cups milk

1 cup chicken or vegetable broth

3 large eggs

1 teaspoon salt

1/2 teaspoon freshly ground black pepper

1/2 teaspoon dried dill

1 pound asparagus

3 to 4 ounces oyster mushrooms, coarsely chopped

1/4 cup thinly sliced shallots

1 cup (4 ounces) shredded Gruyère or Swiss cheese

1. Preheat the oven to 400°F. Spray a 9 × 13–inch baking pan or casserole with nonstick cooking spray.

2. Using a serrated knife, cut the bread into 3/4-inch slices, then stack 4 or 5 slices of bread. Cut them into 3/4-inch cubes. Repeat with the remaining bread and put all of the cubes in a large bowl.

3. In medium bowl, whisk together the milk, broth, eggs, salt, pepper, and dill until combined. Pour the mixture over the bread.

4. Snap off the tough ends of the asparagus and cut the spears into 1-inch pieces. Add them to the bread along with the mushrooms and shallots. Fold everything together well to combine the ingredients. Spoon them into the prepared pan and pat down the top to compact the ingredients. Sprinkle the cheese evenly over the top.

5. Bake the pudding for 45 minutes, or until the top is browned and crisp and there is no liquid in the center. Let it sit for 10 minutes before cutting it into portions.

Stress Saver: Look for frozen asparagus tips and bags of unseasoned bread cubes to save some prep time.

Eye Appeal: Instead of mushrooms, add 1 cup sliced pitted black olives for color contrast and a flavor complement to the asparagus.

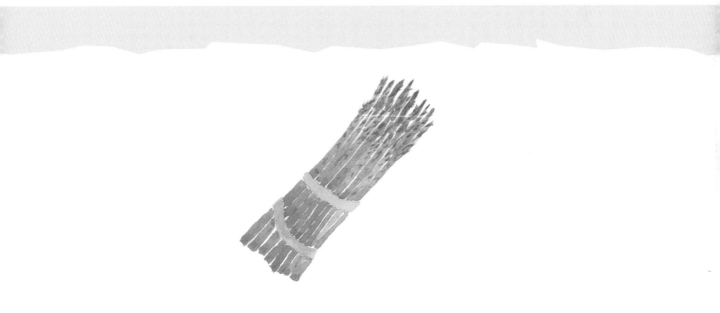

Bistilla (Moroccan Meat Pie)

A classic bistilla is made with layers of phyllo dough encasing a fragrantly spiced meat mixture—often pigeon. You might also find whole hard-boiled eggs inside, and the top is always dusted with confectioners' sugar and cinnamon. Since phyllo can be hard to work with, I have substituted frozen puff pastry here. This meat pie makes a very dramatic presentation, perfect for a dinner party or holiday. It is a sweet-savory balancing act that pairs well with a semi-dry white wine like Riesling.

**HANDS-OFF:
30 MINUTES**

SERVES 6

1/2 cup (2 ounces) whole almonds,
    toasted (see page 151)

3 tablespoons confectioners'
    sugar, divided

2 teaspoons ground cinnamon,
    divided

3 large eggs

1 pound ground turkey

1 cup diced onion

2/3 cup raisins

1/2 cup chopped fresh cilantro

1 teaspoon minced garlic

2 tablespoons freshly squeezed
    lemon juice

1 teaspoon ground ginger

3/4 teaspoon salt

continues on next page

1. Preheat the oven to 400°F. Line a baking sheet with parchment paper.

2. In a food processor, combine the almonds, 2 tablespoons of the sugar, and 1 teaspoon of the cinnamon. Pulse a few times so that there are still chunks of almonds for crunchiness.

3. In a large bowl, whisk the eggs until blended. Take out 1 tablespoon of the eggs and put it in a small dish; set aside. To the remaining eggs, add the turkey, onion, raisins, cilantro, garlic, lemon juice, ginger, salt, pepper, coriander, and saffron. Mix thoroughly to distribute the spices without squashing the meat.

4. Unfold 1 piece of pastry, place it on the prepared pan, and roll it lightly with a rolling pin to smooth the seams. Be careful not to compress the edges. Spread 1/4 cup of the almond mixture over the center of the pastry, then top with half of the turkey mixture. Form the turkey into a log

1/2 teaspoon freshly ground
   black pepper
1/2 teaspoon ground
   coriander
Pinch of saffron threads
One 17.3-ounce package
   puff pastry, thawed in the
   refrigerator

about $3^{1}/_{2}$ inches wide, leaving a 1-inch border at either end of the pastry. Fold 1 long side of the pastry over the turkey. Moisten the other long side with the reserved egg, then fold the other half of the pastry over and press it to seal against the moistened edge. Moisten the ends and press them together as well. Use the parchment to roll the packet, seam-side down, toward one end of the baking sheet. Repeat with the remaining ingredients, making another packet and rolling it to sit at least 2 inches from the other one.

5. Use the tip of a knife to poke 3 holes in the top of each pastry. Bake the bistilla for 30 minutes, until they are puffed and brown. Combine the remaining 1 tablespoon sugar and 1 teaspoon cinnamon and sift them over the top of the rolls. Present the whole rolls and then cut each one in thirds to serve.

casseroles & roasts

Squash and Corn Enchiladas

This is an unusual use for canned pumpkin. Make sure to get the pure-pack pumpkin and not the pie filling. Canned pumpkin is often actually butternut squash, which I thought sounded better in the title than pumpkin enchiladas! I prefer to use corn tortillas for their flavor, but flour tortillas would work here as well. The pecans add a satisfying crunch to the filling.

SERVES 4

One 15-ounce can pure pumpkin

One 15 1/4-ounce can corn with bell
    peppers, drained

1/2 cup diced onion

1/2 cup (2 ounces) pecan pieces,
    toasted (see page 151)

1 tablespoon minced garlic

1 teaspoon ground cumin

1 teaspoon paprika or chili powder

1/2 teaspoon salt

1/2 teaspoon ground cinnamon

Eight 6-inch corn tortillas

One 16-ounce jar salsa verde

1 1/2 cups (6 ounces) shredded pepper
    jack cheese

1. Preheat the oven to 350°F. Spray a 9 × 12–inch casserole with nonstick cooking spray.

2. In a medium bowl, mix together the pumpkin, corn, onion, pecans, garlic, cumin, paprika, salt, and cinnamon. Taste and adjust the seasoning as needed.

3. Spoon a generous 1/3 cup of the mixture in a line down the center of each tortilla, roll it closed, and place seam-side down in the pan. Top the enchiladas with the salsa, spreading it to the edges. Layer the cheese over the top.

4. Bake the enchiladas for 25 minutes, or until the cheese is browned and the filling is hot. Serve 2 enchiladas per person.

Eye Appeal: For a fall color palette, substitute one 15-ounce can of black beans, drained and rinsed, for the corn. You could also add a few leaves of baby spinach on top of the filling before rolling each enchilada.

Enchiladas Suizas

Despite the fancy name, this is a simple baked enchilada casserole. It's based on a recipe by chef Rick Bayless from his cookbook Mexico, One Plate at a Time. *You can vary the spice level greatly by using either tomatoes with chiles or just plain diced tomatoes. You may feel like there's a lot of sauce, but corn tortillas need a lot of liquid to keep them moist.*

**HANDS-OFF:
35 MINUTES**

SERVES 4 TO 5

Two 14¹/2-ounce cans diced tomatoes
    with chiles (or without, as desired)
1 cup diced onion
¹/2 cup light sour cream
3 cups shredded or chopped cooked
    chicken (about 12 ounces; see Note)
Eight to ten 6-inch corn tortillas
1 cup (4 ounces) shredded Monterey
    jack cheese

1. Preheat the oven to 350°F.

2. In a food processor or blender, combine the tomatoes and onion and blend until uniform but still chunky. Add the sour cream and blend.

3. In a medium bowl, mix the chicken with ¹/2 cup of the sauce. In a 9 × 12–inch casserole, spread another ¹/2 cup of the sauce. Spoon about ¹/3 cup chicken in a line down the center of a tortilla, then carefully roll up and place seam-side down in the dish. Repeat with the remaining tortillas and chicken. Pour the remaining sauce over the top and then scatter the cheese over the top.

4. Bake the enchiladas for 30 to 35 minutes, or until they are heated through and bubbling. Let cool for 5 to 10 minutes before serving 2 enchiladas per portion.

Stress Saver: If your tortillas are breaking apart, wrap them in a clean, lightly damp kitchen towel and microwave on high heat for 1 minute. Or, put them in a low (250°F) oven, wrapped in a damp towel, for 10 to 15 minutes. Let them cool slightly before handling.

Eye Appeal: Sprinkle each portion with a little chopped fresh cilantro or parsley or a spoonful of salsa verde or extra sour cream.

Note: Precooked chicken breast strips work well for this and can be found in the meat department of many supermarkets.

Nutty Pumpkin Lasagna

HANDS-OFF:
35 MINUTES

I love lasagna, but it takes a long time to make and bake on a weeknight. So I developed this quicker version, based on a recipe for pumpkin tortelloni by Sonoma, California, chef Carlo Cavallo. The sliced almonds add a buttery crunch, but you could substitute other chopped toasted nuts, depending on what you have on hand and your family likes.

SERVES 6 TO 8

1 cup (4 ounces) sliced almonds

One 8- or 9-ounce box no-boil (oven-ready) lasagna noodles

One 29-ounce can pure pumpkin (not pie filling)

1 cup (4 ounces) shredded Parmesan cheese

1 teaspoon minced garlic

1 1/2 teaspoons dried sage

1 1/2 teaspoons salt

1/2 teaspoon freshly ground black pepper

3/4 cup chicken or vegetable broth, divided

2 cups (8 ounces) shredded mixed Italian cheeses

1. Preheat the oven to 425°F. Spread the almonds on a rimmed baking sheet (jelly-roll pan). Place the pan in the oven while it heats to toast the almonds for 10 to 12 minutes.

2. Put the noodles in a 9 × 13–inch baking dish and pour hot water over them to soak.

3. Meanwhile, in a large bowl, combine the pumpkin, Parmesan, garlic, sage, salt, and pepper. Stir in 3/4 cup of the toasted almonds.

4. Remove the noodles from the baking dish and drain; discard the water. Pour 1/4 cup of the broth into the dish. Put in 1 layer of noodles, then half of the pumpkin mixture, smoothing it to make it even. Put in another layer of noodles and the remaining pumpkin. Top with the final layer of noodles, then sprinkle on the cheese and remaining 1/4 cup almonds. Pour the remaining 1/2 cup stock over the top.

5. Bake the lasagna for 25 minutes, or until it is browned and bubbly. Let stand for 10 minutes before serving.

Baked Polenta with Bacon and Peppers

HANDS-OFF: 25 MINUTES

This is like a baked pasta dish, and makes use of precooked polenta, usually available in 1-pound packages at most grocery stores. You could also use about 4 cups of leftover cooked pasta in place of the polenta, especially if it already has some tomato sauce on it. Precooked bacon is now available in many stores. It is softly cooked, so takes well to additional crisping on the top of a casserole. Make sure to put the bacon and onion just under the cheese so that they get enough direct heat. If you don't want to use bacon, substitute some sliced mushrooms or zucchini.

SERVES 4

One 1-pound package prepared
   polenta
1/4 cup plain or Italian dried bread
   crumbs or panko (see Note)
1/4 teaspoon freshly ground black
   pepper
1 teaspoon minced garlic
1 1/2 cups marinara sauce
1/3 cup chopped roasted bell
   peppers
1/3 cup diced cooked bacon (about
   5 strips)
1/4 cup diced red onion
1/2 cup (2 ounces) grated Parmesan
   cheese or shredded mixed Italian
   cheeses

1. Preheat the oven to 350°F. Spray an 8- or 9-inch casserole with nonstick cooking spray.

2. Cut the polenta into twelve 1/2-inch slices and arrange them in the pan, overlapping if necessary. In a small bowl or measuring cup, combine the bread crumbs and pepper. In another bowl, stir the garlic into the marinara sauce.

3. Top the polenta (in this order) with the peppers, sauce, bacon, onion, cheese, and bread crumb mixture. Bake for 25 minutes, or until the polenta is browned and bubbling. Serve immediately.

Note: Panko are Japanese coarse dried bread crumbs that you can usually find in the Asian section of your grocery or a specialty store. They are crunchier than the fine dried bread crumbs usually found in supermarkets.

Egyptian Macaroni en Crema

According to our friend Nabil Samaan, this is a real comfort food dish in Egypt and one that his mother has made for him many times. I've made the casserole more hands off by cooking the pasta directly in the creamy béchamel sauce rather than boiling it first. You can add other vegetables to this as you like or some ground toasted almonds, as Nabil does. It's a hearty meal with Shredded Carrot Salad (page 20) on the side.

SERVES 8

1 pound ground beef

1 cup diced onion

2 teaspoons ground cinnamon, divided

1 1/2 teaspoons salt, divided

1 teaspoon ground allspice

1/2 teaspoon freshly ground black pepper

5 cups 2% low-fat milk

2 large eggs

1/4 cup all-purpose flour

One 16-ounce box penne or fusilli pasta

3 cups packed baby spinach

1/2 cup fresh bread crumbs

1/2 cup (2 ounces) shredded or grated Parmesan cheese

1. Preheat the oven to 350°F. Spray a deep 9 × 13–inch baking pan with nonstick cooking spray.

2. In a medium bowl, mix together the ground beef, onion, 1 teaspoon of the cinnamon, 1/2 teaspoon of the salt, the allspice, and pepper.

3. In another medium bowl, whisk together the milk, eggs, flour, the remaining 1 teaspoon cinnamon, and the remaining 1 teaspoon salt until combined.

4. Spread the uncooked pasta in the prepared pan. Crumble the beef mixture evenly over the top. Use a spatula to lightly pat down the mixture, but don't pack it. Pour the milk mixture over the top. (It may seem like a lot, but you need the liquid to cook the pasta.) Layer on the spinach, the bread crumbs, and finally the cheese.

5. Bake the casserole for 50 to 55 minutes, or until the noodles are soft and the top is golden and bubbling. Let it sit for 10 to 15 minutes before spooning out portions.

Caramelized-Onion Brisket

This recipe requires a beef brisket with the fat cap still attached. In some areas of the country, that's harder to find than you might expect. But ask the butcher at your market if you don't see one displayed. This is a great recipe for a holiday dinner or weekend meal, when you've got some time to wait for a meltingly delicious roast to slow-cook properly. This one comes out with caramelized onions ready to serve on the side. Just add some Rosemary Yorkshire Pudding (page 27) and a salad and you'll be popular indeed.

**HANDS-OFF:
6 HOURS
40 MINUTES**

SERVES 6 TO 8

1 tablespoon vegetable oil

3 pounds onions, quartered

One 4-pound beef brisket with fat cap intact (see above)

2 teaspoons salt

1 tablespoon paprika

1 tablespoon packed light or dark brown sugar

2 teaspoons minced garlic

1 teaspoon dried thyme

1 teaspoon freshly ground black pepper

1. Preheat the oven to 300°F.

2. In a roasting pan large enough for the brisket to lay flat, toss the oil and onions together. Gather them into a pile in the middle. Lay the brisket, fat side up, on top of the onions, tucking them underneath as much as possible.

3. In a small bowl, mix together the salt, paprika, sugar, garlic, thyme, and pepper. Rub it on the top of the brisket, packing on any remaining.

4. Roast the brisket for about 6 1/2 hours, until a meat thermometer inserted in the center registers at least 200°F and the meat is very tender. Remove the brisket from the oven and let it rest for 10 to 15 minutes before carving it into thick slices. Serve the brisket with some of the onions and juices from the pan. The next day, process any remaining onions and juice in a food processor until finely chopped and spread them on sandwiches made with slices of the leftover roast.

Texas Chili Meat Loaf

HANDS-OFF:
1 HOUR
15 MINUTES

Inspired by the pared-down, beanless chili of Texas, this meat loaf has just a bit of spice and a great glaze. If you're a chilihead, add more chipotle hot sauce to the glaze and meat mixture or use puréed canned chipotles in adobo sauce. If you can get pimentón, which is Spanish smoked paprika, it adds a nice smoky flavor. Serve this with Mason-Dixon Cornbread (page 149) and cold beer.

SERVES 8

Chipotle Glaze

1/4 cup ketchup

2 tablespoons packed light brown
  sugar

2 teaspoons apple cider vinegar

3 shakes chipotle sauce or other hot
  sauce

Meat Loaf

2 pounds ground meat (preferably
  half beef and half turkey)

1 cup yellow or white cornmeal

1/2 cup milk

1/2 cup diced onion

2 large eggs, lightly beaten

1 tablespoon minced garlic

2 tablespoons chili powder

continues on next page

1. Preheat the oven to 350°F.

2. To make the glaze: In a small bowl, mix together the ketchup, sugar, vinegar, and hot sauce. Set aside.

3. To make the meat loaf: In a large bowl, combine the meat, cornmeal, milk, onion, eggs, garlic, chili powder, oregano, salt, pimentón, pepper, Worcestershire sauce, and hot sauce. Mix until evenly blended, without over-kneading the meat.

4. Line a rimmed baking sheet (jelly-roll pan) with aluminum foil. Form the meat mixture into a loaf about 9 inches long and 5 inches wide. Brush the top thickly with the glaze.

1 tablespoon dried oregano

1¹/₂ teaspoons salt

¹/₂ teaspoon hot or sweet pimentón or
paprika

¹/₂ teaspoon freshly ground black pepper

2 teaspoons Worcestershire sauce

¹/₂ teaspoon chipotle sauce or other
hot sauce

5. Bake the meat loaf for about 1 hour, or until an instant-read thermometer inserted in the center of the loaf registers 160°F. Remove from the oven and let cool for 15 to 20 minutes before cutting into slices and serving.

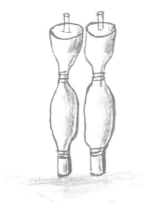

Roasted Root Vegetables

HANDS-OFF:
40 MINUTES

This is one of the simplest meals you can prepare, and a good way to get some vegetables into your diet. Once you start looking, you'll realize how many options you have: red, yellow, and purple potatoes; yams and sweet potatoes; carrots; parsnips; turnips; red, yellow, and striped beets; onions and shallots—the list goes on. I always try to include some peeled garlic cloves. All you need to complete the meal is some Romesco Sauce (recipe follows), a tomato-based sauce from Spain, and a bit of crusty bread. You can also serve the Romesco Sauce with the Spanish Omelette (page 65), as a sandwich spread with any kind of meat, swirled into a brothy soup, or dolloped on grilled fish. Basically, you should never be without some Romesco Sauce in your refrigerator!

**SERVES 3 TO 4 AS A MAIN DISH
OR 6 TO 8 AS A SIDE DISH**

2 pounds assorted root vegetables, such as potatoes, sweet potatoes, carrots, parsnips, turnips, and beets, trimmed and cut into bite-sized pieces (about 8 cups)

1 onion or 3 shallots, cut into wedges

2 tablespoons olive oil

Salt and freshly ground black pepper, to taste

1 teaspoon dried rosemary, oregano, or thyme

1. Preheat the oven to 450°F.

2. In a large bowl, toss together the vegetables, onion, and oil. Spread them on a rimmed baking sheet (jelly-roll pan). Sprinkle the top generously with salt, pepper, and herbs.

3. Roast the vegetables for 40 minutes, or until a knife inserted in a large piece goes in easily. Serve the vegetables immediately with romesco sauce or mayonnaise on the side.

Stress Saver: Some supermarkets now sell bags of peeled and cubed beets and sweet potatoes, which make really quick work of this recipe.

Romesco Sauce

MAKES ABOUT 2 CUPS

1/2 cup (2 ounces) raw almonds

One 141/2-ounce can diced tomatoes, drained

1/4 cup oil-packed or moist sun-dried tomatoes

1 egg yolk (see Note)

2 tablespoons balsamic vinegar

1 teaspoon Vietnamese chili-garlic sauce (see Note)

1 teaspoon minced garlic

1/2 teaspoon salt

1/8 teaspoon cayenne pepper

1/3 cup olive oil

1. Preheat the oven to 350°F.

2. Toast the almonds on a rimmed baking sheet (jelly-roll pan) until they are fairly dark but not black, about 12 minutes. Remove immediately from the sheet.

3. In a food processor, finely grind the almonds, then add the canned tomatoes, sun-dried tomatoes, egg yolk, vinegar, chili-garlic sauce, garlic, salt, and cayenne. Blend until smooth. With the processor running, slowly add the olive oil until the mixture is emulsified. Taste and adjust the seasoning as desired.

4. Refrigerate the romesco for at least 15 minutes for the flavors to come together. It keeps, covered and refrigerated, for 2 weeks.

Notes: Chili-garlic sauce is a chunky Vietnamese mixture of red chiles, garlic, and vinegar. You can usually find it in a jar in the Asian section of large groceries or in any Asian-foods store.

Young children, the elderly, and those with suppressed immune systems may want to avoid raw eggs. You can substitute an equivalent amount of pasteurized egg product (see the package for measurement) or simply omit the egg yolk, although it helps to emulsify the sauce.

Peanutty Cabbage ROLLs

HANDS-OFF: 20 MINUTES

If you've been looking for a recipe for tofu that isn't fried or squashy, try this one. It's a take-off on Tahu Goreng, *from the* Moosewood Restaurant Daily Special *cookbook, and even people suspicious of tofu will like it. The filling is good in any kind of wrapper—from pita to tortilla to plain lettuce. One of the best is eggroll wrappers, which neatly enclose the filling. Look for them in the refrigerated produce section of your grocery or an Asian foods store. If you're faced with determined anti-tofu eaters, then substitute an equal amount of shredded cooked chicken for the tofu.*

SERVES 4 AS AN ENTRÉE OR 8 AS AN APPETIZER

1/3 cup smooth peanut butter

4 tablespoons low-sodium soy sauce, divided

4 tablespoons freshly squeezed lime juice, divided

2 tablespoons honey

2 tablespoons vegetable oil, plus extra as needed

1 tablespoon rice wine vinegar or sherry vinegar

1 to 2 teaspoons chili-garlic sauce (see Note, page 89)

2 teaspoons minced garlic, divided

1 teaspoon cumin seeds, divided

continues on next page

1. Preheat the oven to 350°F. Spray a 9 × 13–inch casserole with nonstick cooking spray.

2. In a medium bowl or a blender, whisk together or blend the peanut butter, 2 tablespoons of the soy sauce, 2 tablespoons of the lime juice, the honey, oil, vinegar, chili-garlic sauce, 1 teaspoon of the garlic, and 1/2 teaspoon of the cumin until fairly smooth. Set aside.

3. In a food processor, combine the tofu, mushrooms, broth, remaining 2 tablespoons soy sauce, remaining 2 tablespoons lime juice, remaining 1 teaspoon garlic, and remaining 1/2 teaspoon cumin. Pulse 8 to 10 times, until the mixture is chunky. Remove the mixture to a bowl and stir in the cabbage and peanuts.

4. Take one wrapper and spoon about 1/4 cup of the tofu filling into the center. Roll the wrapper over the filling

8 ounces firm tofu, drained

3 ounces oyster or shiitake mushrooms, coarsely chopped (1 cup)

1/4 cup vegetable broth

3 cups shredded Napa cabbage

1/2 cup unsalted peanuts

12 eggroll wrappers

Chopped fresh cilantro, for garnish

once, fold in the sides, and roll up the wrapper like a burrito. Place in the casserole, seam-side down. Repeat with the remaining filling and wrappers. Brush the tops of the rolls with oil to help them crisp in the oven.

5. Bake the rolls for 20 to 25 minutes, or until the filling is heated through. Serve the warm rolls drizzled with some of the sauce and garnished with chopped cilantro.

Medium-Rare Greek Meat Loaf

Unless you're making a long-cooked dish like Lamb Tagine (page 53) or Wine-Braised Lamb Shanks (page 112), it's usually best to cook it medium-rare. The tender pink in the middle keeps the meat juicy and flavorful. This meat loaf is based on that idea and adds the flavors of classic Greek lamb chops. The chickpeas make an attractive pattern studding slices of this loaf. Serve with the Greek Leek and Greens Pie (page 69) for a theme dinner, or with simple Roasted Root Vegetables (page 88) on the side.

SERVES 8

2 large eggs

2 pounds ground lamb

One 15-ounce can chickpeas, drained and rinsed

1 1/2 cups diced red or yellow onion

3/4 cup fresh bread crumbs

1 tablespoon minced garlic

1 lemon, zested

2 tablespoons minced fresh rosemary, or 2 teaspoons dried rosemary, divided

2 teaspoons salt

Freshly ground black pepper, to taste

1. Preheat the oven to 400°F. Line a rimmed baking sheet (jelly-roll pan) with aluminum foil and spray the foil with nonstick cooking spray.

2. In a large bowl, whisk the eggs until blended. Add the lamb, chickpeas, onion, bread crumbs, garlic, zest, half of the rosemary, and the salt. Mix well without overly squashing the meat. On the prepared pan, form the mixture into a loaf about 9 inches long, 5 inches wide, and no more than 2 1/2 inches thick. Pat any loose chickpeas and onions on top, then the remaining rosemary. Generously grind pepper over the top.

3. Bake the meat loaf for 1 hour, or until a meat thermometer inserted in the center registers 150°F for medium-rare. The lamb should still be a little pink in the middle. Let it sit for 10 minutes before you cut it into thick slices and serve.

Fish Veracruz

Veracruz sauce is a classic preparation from the Caribbean coast of Mexico. It combines ingredients imported by the Spanish conquerors with native ingredients. This is a much quicker version of the dish, making use of convenient ingredients like canned roasted tomatoes and chopped pitted olives. Serve it with packaged yellow rice or plain white rice.

SERVES 6

1 tablespoon olive oil

One 28-ounce can fire-roasted or whole plum tomatoes

1 1/2 cups diced onion

1 cup chopped fresh parsley

1/2 cup chopped pitted black Greek or kalamata olives

2 tablespoons drained capers (rinsed if salt packed)

2 pickled jalapeño chiles or pepperoncini, coarsely chopped, plus 1 tablespoon of the pickling liquid

2 teaspoons minced garlic

2 bay leaves

1 teaspoon dried oregano

1/2 teaspoon salt, plus more to taste

1/4 teaspoon freshly ground black pepper, plus more to taste

2 pounds firm, meaty fish fillets like halibut, salmon, or snapper

1. Preheat the oven to 350°F. Rub a 9 × 12–inch casserole with the oil.

2. Break up the tomatoes with your hands, letting them fall into the casserole. Add the onion, parsley, olives, capers, jalapeños and pickling liquid, garlic, bay leaves, oregano, salt, and pepper. Stir to combine the ingredients. Nestle the fish into the sauce and sprinkle with additional salt and pepper.

3. Bake the casserole for 25 to 30 minutes, or until the fish is just opaque all the way through, there are white droplets on the surface of the fish, and the sauce is bubbling. Serve each portion of fish with a generous spoonful of sauce.

Ratatouille-Stuffed Baked Onions

HANDS-OFF:
1 HOUR

Ratatouille is a French dish of tomatoes, zucchini, eggplant, onion, and garlic simmered together to make a chunky sauce. I've used the basic ingredients here to fill hollowed-out red onions for a beautiful vegetarian dish that's very low in fat. My friend Chris Cosentino, chef at Incanto in San Francisco, showed me the trick of using a melon baller to hollow the onions. I have served this with Cheesy Yummy Baked Polenta (page 24) or Sausage Strata (page 68). A green salad would also be a nice accompaniment.

SERVES 4

4 large red onions (about 12 ounces each)

1 small eggplant (6 to 8 ounces)

1 small zucchini

One 14^{1}/2-ounce can diced tomatoes

^{1}/2 cup chopped fresh basil

^{1}/4 cup chopped roasted bell peppers

2 teaspoons minced garlic

1 teaspoon salt

^{1}/4 teaspoon red pepper flakes

^{1}/2 cup dried bread crumbs

2 tablespoons olive oil

1 teaspoon dried oregano

1. Preheat the oven to 375°F.

2. Trim the root end of each onion so it sits flat. Trim off about ^{3}/4 inch from the top and remove the papery skin. Use the large end of a melon baller to scoop out the middle of each onion, leaving about 2 layers of onion on the sides and bottom. Use the scoop to smooth the inside edges where possible. Stand the onions in a 9-inch square or round casserole so that they fit fairly snugly.

3. Trim and quarter the eggplant and zucchini lengthwise. Cut them crosswise into ^{1}/4-inch slices. In a large bowl, combine the eggplant, zucchini, tomatoes, basil, peppers, garlic, salt, and pepper flakes. Fill each onion with this mixture and mound the filling above the tops. Any leftover filling can be placed around the onions in the casserole.

4. In a small bowl, mix together the bread crumbs, oil, and oregano. Spoon onto the tops of the onions and pat down lightly.

5. Bake the onions for 1 hour, or until they are tender and the filling is bubbling. Serve immediately, spooning any sauce in the casserole over them.

Hands-Off Technique: Gather the shards of onion scooped out of the centers and pulse them briefly in a food processor. Refrigerate for up to 4 days in a heavy self-sealing plastic bag for use in other recipes.

Broiled Margarita Chicken

Margaritas have an alluring salty-sour flavor with a touch of sweetness. This recipe uses the basic margarita ingredients to make a flavorful sauce for chicken. If you think you'd like a slightly sweeter sauce, try substituting orange juice for 2 tablespoons of the lime juice. The sauce does not taste alcoholic—most of the alcohol evaporates during cooking. Serve this over hot rice or quinoa.

SERVES 4

1 tablespoon vegetable oil

4 boneless, skinless chicken breasts
  (about 1 3/4 pounds total)

1 teaspoon ground cumin

1/2 teaspoon salt

1/4 teaspoon freshly ground black
  pepper

1 cup diced onion

1/2 cup freshly squeezed lime juice

1/2 cup chicken broth

1/4 cup tequila

1 tablespoon honey

1 tablespoon all-purpose flour

1 teaspoon minced garlic

Coarse sea salt, for garnish

1. Preheat the broiler.

2. Add the oil to a 9 × 12–inch casserole. Turn the chicken in the oil to coat it, then sprinkle the top with the cumin, salt, and pepper. Sprinkle the onion around the chicken.

3. In a small bowl, combine the juice, broth, tequila, honey, flour, and garlic. Stir to dissolve the honey and flour, then pour the liquid over and around the chicken.

4. Broil the chicken about 5 inches from the heat source for 20 to 25 minutes, until it is browned on top and no longer pink on the bottom. Sprinkle each serving with a pinch of sea salt for the complete margarita experience.

Hands-Off Technique: Measure the honey with the same spoon you used to measure the oil. It will slide right out of the oiled spoon.

Roasted Asian Pesto Fish

HANDS-OFF: 20 MINUTES

If you don't like cooking fish on the stove top because of the smell, this is a great alternative. The final dish has a bright green color and a lively flavor. It is just as good cold for a light meal as it is hot from the oven. My favorite fish for this recipe is wild Alaska salmon, but any meaty fish should work well. It makes a lovely meal accompanied with Bread Salad (page 15) or Ants Climbing a Tree (page 137).

SERVES 6 TO 8

3 cups fresh cilantro leaves

1 bunch scallions, including 4 inches of green parts, cut into 1-inch pieces (about 1½ cups)

4 tablespoons olive oil, divided

1 serrano chile, seeded

2 tablespoons crushed ginger from a jar

1 tablespoon minced garlic

2 tablespoons rice vinegar

1 teaspoon salt

½ teaspoon freshly ground black pepper

2 pounds wild Alaska salmon fillets, pin bones removed

¼ cup sesame seeds (optional)

1. Preheat the oven to 350°F.

2. In a food processor, combine the cilantro, scallions, 3 tablespoons of the oil, the chile, ginger, garlic, vinegar, salt, and pepper. Process until the mixture is well puréed. Scrape the sides down with a rubber spatula. Taste and adjust the seasoning. Process again briefly if needed. The pesto should be a little salty to flavor the fish.

3. Line a rimmed baking sheet (jelly-roll pan) with aluminum foil and rub the foil with the remaining 1 tablespoon oil. Rub the top and bottom sides of the fish in the oil. Place the fish skin-side down and spread the pesto evenly on top. Sprinkle with the sesame seeds (if using).

4. Bake for 20 minutes, or until the fish is tender and still slightly translucent pink in the center. Serve immediately with rice, or refrigerate the fish until it is chilled and serve it cold.

Pomegranate-Almond Chicken

Pomegranate juice is now widely available and is reported to be quite good for us, too. It's a beautiful cranberry-colored liquid, and the best brands are translucent, not cloudy. This recipe was developed after eating some delicious chicken kebabs in a restaurant in San Francisco called Medjool. They specialize in Mediterranean small plates, and the chicken was served with a syrupy pomegranate sauce that had almonds in it. This version is a bit different, of course, since it's hands off, but hopefully you'll enjoy the sweet-spicy bite of the sauce and a new way of flavoring chicken. Serve this as an entrée with couscous or as part of a collection of appetizers with squares of Spanish Omelette (page 65) and Charleston Chicken-Pecan Salad (page 19) spread on croutons.

HANDS-OFF: 45 MINUTES (INCLUDING MARINATING TIME)

SERVES 4 AS AN ENTRÉE OR 8 AS AN APPETIZER

About 1¼ pounds boneless, skinless chicken thighs or breasts

½ cup pomegranate juice

¼ cup honey

2 tablespoons freshly squeezed lemon juice

1 tablespoon olive oil

1 tablespoon minced garlic

1 teaspoon ground ginger

continues on next page

1. In a large, self-sealing plastic bag, combine the chicken, pomegranate juice, honey, lemon juice, oil, garlic, ginger, cumin, paprika, salt, and cayenne. Seal the bag and massage it to combine the ingredients well. Set the bag aside at room temperature for at least 30 minutes or refrigerate it for up to 3 hours.

2. Preheat the broiler. Line a broiler pan or a rimmed baking sheet (jelly-roll pan) with aluminum foil and spray the foil with nonstick cooking spray.

1 teaspoon ground cumin

1/2 teaspoon sweet paprika

1/2 teaspoon salt

1/4 teaspoon cayenne pepper
  (optional)

2 tablespoons creamy almond
  butter

3. Using tongs, carefully remove the chicken from the marinade and place it in a single layer on the prepared pan. Broil it about 5 inches from the heat source for 15 to 20 minutes, or until the chicken is browned and cooked through. Leave it whole to serve as an entrée or cut it into chunks for appetizers.

4. Meanwhile, pour the marinade into a saucepan or skillet and bring it to a simmer. Cook it for about 10 minutes. Whisk in the almond butter until smooth. Serve each portion of chicken with some of the sauce drizzled over it.

Eye Appeal: If you can find a fresh pomegranate, garnish this dish with some of the beautiful jewel-like seeds.

Backyard Camp-Out Dinner

This easy, self-contained dish is perfect for backyard parties or making ahead and cooking as needed. The plentiful sauce produced during cooking is great over a bed of couscous or rice or sopped up with some crusty bread. If you're having a party, assemble batches of these ahead of time and cook them to order as people arrive. Use wide heavy-duty aluminum foil or a double thickness of regular foil to prevent leaks.

SERVES 4

1 1/2 pounds firm, white-fleshed fish
fillets, such as halibut, mahi mahi,
or sea bass

Salt and freshly ground black pepper,
to taste

2 pinches red pepper flakes

1 large leek, halved lengthwise,
well rinsed, and thinly sliced,
white part only

1 cup cherry tomatoes, halved if
large

1/2 cup chopped fresh basil or parsley
(or both)

1/2 cup dry white wine

2 tablespoons balsamic vinegar

1 tablespoon unsalted butter, cubed,
or olive oil

1. Light a medium-hot indirect fire in a charcoal grill or preheat a gas grill to 350°F.

2. Tear off two 24-inch lengths of heavy-duty foil. Spray them with nonstick cooking spray. Bend up a 1-inch margin all around the edges to hold in the liquid.

3. Put half of the fillets on each piece of foil and sprinkle them with salt, pepper, and a pinch of red pepper flakes. Divide the leeks, tomatoes, and herbs between the packets. Mix the wine and vinegar in a measuring cup and pour half of the liquid over each packet of fillets, then scatter half of the butter over each. Bring the long sides of the foil edges together and fold them over to seal the packets well. Use the ends to make a handle at the top if you can, for easy transport. Cook now, or refrigerate the packets until needed, up to 12 hours.

4. Grill the packets over indirect heat, with the grill covered, for 25 minutes, or until the fish is cooked through and the leeks are tender. Peek inside one packet if necessary to determine doneness, though you don't really need to.

5. Open each packet carefully and divide its contents between 2 plates. Spoon the sauce over the fish and vegetables and serve immediately.

Catalan Chicken

HANDS-OFF:
30 MINUTES

A restaurant in San Francisco called B44 serves wonderful Spanish food, including a roasted rabbit dish with almond sauce. I tested the recipe to standardize it for a magazine and liked it so much I developed this hands-off version using chicken. Believe me, the original recipe is not hands off, although it is incredibly delicious. Hopefully you'll enjoy this version if you can't have the real deal at B44. Serve it over couscous or rice mixed with raisins.

SERVES 6

1 tablespoon extra-virgin olive oil

1 1/2 pounds boneless, skinless chicken thighs

Salt

Freshly ground black pepper

1/2 onion, cut into 3 or 4 pieces

1/2 cup (2 ounces) raw unsalted sliced almonds, plus extra for garnish

1/2 cup chopped fresh parsley

1/4 cup fresh bread crumbs

continues on next page

1. Preheat the oven to 400°F.

2. Pour the oil into a 9 × 12–inch casserole and coat the chicken in it on both sides. Sprinkle the chicken with salt and pepper and arrange in a single layer.

3. In a food processor, combine the onion, almonds, parsley, bread crumbs, garlic, vinegar, tomato paste, brandy, thyme, and 1 teaspoon salt. Purée well, scraping down the sides with a rubber spatula if necessary. Spread the purée evenly over and around the chicken. Pour the broth over the top.

1 teaspoon minced garlic

1/4 cup red wine vinegar

2 tablespoons tomato paste

1 tablespoon brandy

1/4 teaspoon dried thyme

11/2 cups chicken broth

4. Bake the chicken for 30 minutes, or until it is cooked through. Serve it immediately over couscous or rice to soak up the sauce, with extra sliced almonds for garnish.

Stress Saver: Buy tomato paste in a tube so that you don't have leftovers from a can (check the package for the correct substitution quantity). Or, measure out tablespoons of leftover tomato paste and freeze them in an ice tray. Then just pop the frozen cubes into a self-sealing plastic bag and keep them frozen until you need them!

Orange Marmalade Chicken

HANDS-OFF:
50 MINUTES
(INCLUDING
MARINATING
TIME)

This recipe was developed years ago when I lived in Washington, D.C. It's still popular with my friend Tom Fox, a culinarily challenged lawyer. You can't get too much easier than 10 minutes of prep, and then you just leave the chicken to marinate until you're ready to cook it. Serve it ultra–hands off with deli mashed potatoes or Asian noodles. It's also pretty tasty with Savory Asparagus Bread Pudding (page 72).

SERVES 4 TO 5

1 to 1 1/2 pounds boneless,
　skinless chicken breasts
　or thighs
1/2 cup orange marmalade
2 tablespoons low-sodium
　soy sauce
1 lime, juiced
1 teaspoon minced garlic
Freshly ground black pepper,
　to taste

1. In a large self-sealing plastic bag, combine the chicken, marmalade, soy sauce, lime juice, garlic, and a generous grinding of pepper. Seal the bag and massage it to distribute the marinade ingredients. Set the bag aside at room temperature for at least 30 minutes or refrigerate it for up to 10 hours. Remove from the refrigerator 15 minutes before cooking if chilled.

2. When you're ready to cook, preheat the broiler. Line a rimmed baking sheet (jelly-roll pan) with aluminum foil and spray the foil with nonstick cooking spray.

3. Carefully remove the chicken from the marinade and place the pieces 1 inch apart on the prepared pan; press the chicken to flatten slightly. Pour some of the marinade over each piece and discard the rest.

4. Broil the chicken about 5 inches from the heat source for 15 to 20 minutes, or until it is browned and cooked through. Remove from the broiler but leave on the pan for 5 minutes to rest. Serve each piece with some of the sauce from the pan.

Pork Roast with Apple Chutney

This is a great recipe for a dinner party, as it makes its own sauce while you straighten the house and set the table. There's plenty of chutney for eight people and leftover pork for sandwiches the next day. Two dinners in one! Serve this with Irish Soda Bread (page 153) and braised greens.

HANDS-OFF:
**1 HOUR
40 MINUTES**

**SERVES 6 TO 8,
WITH LEFTOVERS**

One 3- to 4-pound boneless pork loin roast (not tenderloin)

1 tablespoon minced garlic

1 teaspoon salt

1 teaspoon freshly ground black pepper

4 cups peeled and chopped apples (2 or 3 large), such as Gala or Jonathan

2 heaping cups diced onions

1 cup packed light brown sugar

1 cup raisins or chopped dried fruit (such as apricots or cherries)

1 tablespoon crushed ginger from a jar

1 teaspoon red pepper flakes

1 cup apple cider vinegar

1 cup chicken broth

1. Preheat the oven to 450°F.

2. Rub the pork all over with the garlic and sprinkle it with the salt and pepper.

3. In a large bowl, mix together the apples, onions, sugar, raisins, ginger, and red pepper flakes. Toss well and scrape the mixture into a stainless-steel roasting pan. Mound the mixture in the middle of the pan. Set the pork on top and pour the vinegar and broth around it.

4. Roast for 1 1/2 hours, or until an instant-read thermometer inserted in the center of the roast registers 145°F (if you're using a smaller roast, check the temperature after 1 hour).

5. Using tongs, transfer the pork to a cutting board to rest for 10 to 15 minutes. Scrape the chutney into a bowl. Slice the pork and pass the warm chutney at the table.

Eye Appeal: Use some brightly colored dried fruit, such as cranberries or cherries, to add color to the chutney.

Perfect Pot Roast

HANDS-OFF: 2¹/₂ HOURS

My mother regularly made pot roast when I was growing up, and I still love it. But it always seemed like too much trouble. Come to find out, it's really not! *Make this for guests or a weekend dinner and your house will smell wonderful. You need a heavy Dutch oven with a lid. They are usually made of cast iron and are sometimes enameled as well. The heaviness of their construction allows for slow, even heating. The sweet roasted garlic cloves should definitely be eaten with the meat, which is a great partner for Roasted German Potato Salad (page 16).*

SERVES 4 TO 6

1 tablespoon olive oil

1 tablespoon plus 1 teaspoon sweet or hot paprika or pimentón

1 teaspoon salt

One 2- to 3-pound boneless chuck roast

2 bell peppers, seeded

2 onions or one 10-ounce bag frozen pearl onions

3 medium carrots

8 or more garlic cloves, peeled

One 8-ounce can tomato sauce

1 cup dry red wine

Freshly ground black pepper, to taste

1. Preheat the oven to 300°F.

2. Pour the oil into a large, heavy Dutch oven and put it in the oven to heat.

3. On a dinner plate, mix together the paprika and salt. Roll the roast in it to coat all sides. Cut the peppers and onions lengthwise and the carrots crosswise into 1/4-inch slices. Remove the pot from the oven and carefully add the roast. Scatter the peppers, onions, carrots, and garlic around the roast, then pour in the tomato sauce and wine. Generously grind pepper on top.

4. Cover the pot with a lid or aluminum foil and cook the pot roast for 2¹/2 hours, or until very tender. Transfer the roast to a cutting board and slice. Serve each portion with some vegetables and sauce.

Hands-Off Technique: To defat the sauce, strain it into a heatproof bowl or measuring cup. Let the sauce settle for 10 to 15 minutes to let the fat rise to the top. Skim off as much as you can and then serve the defatted sauce.

Carolina Pulled Pork

This really takes only 5 minutes to prep for the oven! You'll probably be done before the oven is preheated. Pulled pork is a specialty of North Carolina, where I went to college and learned to love this Southern staple on sandwiches, topped with coleslaw. For a small amount of work, you get an incredibly juicy jumble of meat that's perfect for a weekend dinner or party potluck. Serve leftovers (if there are any) on white bread with Red Cabbage Slaw (page 14) for a satisfying lunch.

SERVES 6 (OR 4 CAROLINIANS)

One 3- to 4-pound boneless Boston butt (pork shoulder), excess fat trimmed

Salt and freshly ground black pepper

2 cups (one 19-ounce bottle) tomato-based barbecue sauce

Red pepper flakes or cayenne pepper, to taste (optional)

1 cup apple cider vinegar

1. Preheat the oven to 400°F.

2. Remove any strings or net on the meat. Sprinkle it all over with salt and pepper. Put the pork in a large, heavy pot like a Dutch oven. Taste the barbecue sauce and add red pepper flakes if it isn't spicy enough for you. Pour the vinegar on top of the meat, then the barbecue sauce.

3. Cover the pot and braise the pork in the oven for 3 1/2 to 4 hours, or until the meat is falling apart and shreds very easily when pushed with a spoon. Remove the pot and shred the meat by pushing it against the pot. Stir it together with the sauce.

4. If you want, you can pour the meat and sauce into a colander set over a bowl to drain off any excess fat. The meat will have absorbed most of the sauce already.

5. Serve immediately, with Hoppin' Bob (page 22) and Mason-Dixon Cornbread (page 149), or as a sandwich.

Tandoorish Chicken

**HANDS-OFF:
AT LEAST
6 HOURS
40 MINUTES**

My friends Alex and Veronica Stanich run a restaurant in Sri Lanka, and this recipe is based on one of Alex's dishes, with his clever title borrowed. Like traditional tandoori chicken, the meat is marinated in a yogurt-based sauce and then cooked. It's a great dish for preparing the night or morning before, since you need to marinate it for at least 6 hours. Shredded off the bone, this chicken makes great leftovers, so you might want to double the recipe.

SERVES 4 TO 6

2 pounds bone-in chicken
   thighs
1 cup plain low-fat or whole
   yogurt
1/2 cup coarsely chopped onion
2 tablespoons freshly squeezed
   lime juice
1 tablespoon garam masala
   (see Note, page 126)
1 tablespoon ground cumin
1 teaspoon salt
1 teaspoon minced garlic
1 teaspoon crushed ginger
   from a jar
1/2 canned chipotle in adobo
   sauce or several dashes hot
   sauce

1. Pull off the skin from the chicken and put the chicken in a baking dish or casserole large enough to hold it in a single layer.

2. In a blender or food processor, combine the yogurt, onion, lime juice, garam masala, cumin, salt, garlic, ginger, and chipotle. Blend until smooth. Pour the marinade evenly over the chicken, turning each piece to coat it. Cover and refrigerate the chicken for at least 6 hours or up to 24 hours.

3. Preheat the oven to 400°F. Uncover the chicken and turn each piece over once to coat it. Transfer the dish to the oven and bake for 40 minutes, or until the chicken is opaque throughout. Serve over rice or couscous, with some of the sauce.

Eye Appeal: Scatter each serving with chopped fresh cilantro or parsley for extra color.

Note: To make it with boneless, skinless chicken, cook it for only 30 minutes.

Lasagna with Vegetable Noodles

**HANDS-OFF:
1 HOUR
15 MINUTES**

I was always trying to get more vegetables in my lasagna, and I finally realized that I could just take out the noodles! That leaves more room for thin strips of colorful vegetables like eggplant, zucchini, and summer squash. You don't have to precook them either, as you do with most noodles. It may seem like there's a lot of basil, but the flavor mellows and permeates the dish for a fresh, bright result.

SERVES 8

2½ pounds Japanese or globe eggplants, zucchini, and summer squash

3 tablespoons olive oil

2 teaspoons minced garlic

1¼ teaspoons salt, divided

2 pounds low-fat ricotta cheese

1 large egg, lightly beaten

1 teaspoon dried oregano

4 cups or one 28-ounce jar marinara sauce

continues on next page

1. Preheat the oven to 375°F.

2. If using globe eggplant, peel it since the skin tends to be tough. Cut the vegetables lengthwise into 1/4- to 1/2-inch-thick slices. Put them in a 9 × 13–inch baking pan or casserole with the oil, garlic, and 1 teaspoon of the salt. Carefully toss to coat the vegetables, then transfer them to a plate, leaving any oil and garlic in the pan.

3. In a large bowl, fold together the ricotta, egg, oregano, and the remaining 1/4 teaspoon salt until combined.

4. Spread about 1/2 cup sauce in the bottom of the pan. Top it with a layer of vegetable strips, cutting pieces to fit, then half of the ricotta mixture, 3/4 cup of the sauce,

8 ounces sweet or hot Italian
   sausage (optional), removed
   from casings and crumbled, or
   chopped
1 bunch fresh basil, stemmed
1 cup (4 ounces) shredded mixed
   Italian cheeses

and half of the sausage. Top with half of the basil leaves, spreading them evenly. Make another layer of vegetables, ricotta, and basil, but not the sausage. Top with the remaining vegetables. Top with the remaining sauce and sausage. Scatter the cheeses evenly over the top.

5. Bake the lasagna for 1 hour, or until heated through and the vegetables are crisp-tender but not soft. Remove the lasagna from the oven and let rest for 15 minutes before cutting it into portions.

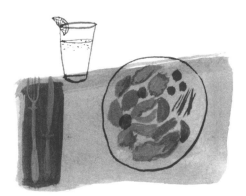

Wine-Braised Lamb Shanks

Braising lamb in a flavorful liquid results in fork-tender meat and a rich sauce. Add some vegetables to the braise and you practically have a complete meal. Having the bones cracked by the butcher allows the meat to fit into the pot better and the marrow helps to thicken the sauce. This is an impressive dish for company, as well as being comfort food on a cold night. Serve it with some quick-cooking couscous and crusty bread to mop up the juices.

HANDS-OFF: 2¹/₂ HOURS

SERVES 4 TO 6

2 cups diced bell peppers

2 cups diced onions

2 cups thinly sliced fennel or carrots

One 14¹/₂-ounce can diced tomatoes

2 tablespoons tomato paste

2 tablespoons all-purpose flour

2 tablespoons packed brown sugar

1 tablespoon minced garlic

continues on next page

1. Preheat the oven to 350°F.

2. In a large, heavy Dutch oven or small roasting pan, stir together the peppers, onions, fennel, tomatoes, tomato paste, flour, sugar, garlic, and cinnamon stick.

3. Rub the shanks with salt and pepper and lay them on top of the vegetables, nestling them into a single layer if possible. Pour the wine over the top.

4. Cover the pan with a lid or aluminum foil and braise for 2¹/₂ hours in the oven, or until the meat comes easily off the bone. Taste the sauce and adjust the seasoning as needed. Remove and discard the cinnamon stick. Serve

One 3-inch cinnamon stick

4 lamb shanks, bones cracked by the butcher

Salt and freshly ground black pepper

2 cups dry red wine

each piece of shank with some of the vegetables and sauce.

Eye Appeal: If you buy fennel with the greens attached, save some of the feathery leaves to mince and sprinkle on top of the shanks before serving.

Baked Salmon in Puff Pastry (Coulibiac)

**HANDS-OFF:
35 MINUTES**

Coulibiac originated as a Russian dish, but was adopted by French chefs as an elegant fish presentation. You may see it made with shredded cooked salmon, but this version uses fillets. They turn out moist and tender, with lots of flavor from the seasonings. Serve this hot or leftover as a cold picnic lunch. You can prepare the uncooked coulibiac ahead of time, wrap it, and refrigerate for up to 24 hours. Then remove it from the refrigerator 15 to 20 minutes before baking.

SERVES 4 TO 6

1/4 cup couscous

Salt

1/3 cup chicken or vegetable broth

One 17.3-ounce package frozen
   puff pastry, thawed in the
   refrigerator

1 large egg, lightly beaten

1 pound salmon fillets, skin and
   pin bones removed

Freshly ground black pepper

2 tablespoons fresh thyme, or
   2 teaspoons dried thyme

2 teaspoons minced garlic

1 lemon, thinly sliced and seeded

1 cup (3 ounces) sliced
   oyster mushrooms

1 whole shallot, thinly sliced

1. Preheat the oven to 400°F. Line a baking sheet with parchment paper.

2. In a small bowl, combine the couscous and 1/8 teaspoon salt. In a microwave on high or on the stove top, heat the broth to almost boiling. Pour it over the couscous; cover and set aside for 5 minutes.

3. Lay 1 square of pastry on the prepared pan. Brush the egg along one edge, then overlap it by 1/2 inch with the other square of pastry to make a rectangle about 18 inches long. Press lightly to seal them together.

4. Stir the couscous, then spread it in a strip about 31/2 inches wide down the center length of the pastry rectangle, leaving a 3/4-inch margin at each end.

5. Season both sides of the salmon with salt and pepper, then lay it on top of the couscous, in a single layer if there is more than 1 fillet. Sprinkle the salmon with the thyme and garlic. Layer the lemon slices on top (you may not need all of them; save the remainder to garnish the plates), then the mushrooms and shallot. Gently stretch one of the long sides of pastry up and halfway over the mushrooms. Brush the edge with egg. Stretch the other long side of the pastry up to overlap the first by about 1/2 inch. Press lightly to seal. Brush the ends with egg and press together to seal; brush the entire surface lightly with the remaining egg. If the pastry has gotten very soft at this point, refrigerate the coulibiac for 15 minutes before proceeding. This will help the pastry to puff.

6. Bake for 30 minutes, or until the pastry is puffed and brown. Let cool for 5 to 10 minutes before slicing into portions.

Garlic-Roasted Chicken with Orange

HANDS-OFF:
1 HOUR
25 MINUTES

Having only a few people for Thanksgiving or a dinner party? Then this is the perfect recipe for you. It cooks in much less time than a large turkey, and the meat will be incredibly moist and flavorful. Or, just make it for yourself and shred the leftover meat to make Charleston Chicken-Pecan Salad (page 19). The best part of making this for a party, though, is that it needs to rest before carving, so you can have it ready when your guests arrive. Scatter chopped root vegetables in the pan to roast alongside, or serve with Cranberry-Ginger Dressing (page 29) and Better than Mom's Apple Pie (page 158) for dessert!

SERVES 4 TO 6

One 4- to 5-pound chicken

2 tablespoons unsalted butter

2 teaspoons honey

Salt and freshly ground black pepper

6 to 8 garlic cloves, peeled (optional)

2 oranges, cut in half

1. Preheat the oven to 400°F. Prepare a roasting pan with a rack (use a roasting "V" rack or a flat cooling rack that fits in the bottom of the pan).

2. Rinse the chicken inside and out and pat it dry. Combine the butter and honey in a cup and microwave on high for 30 seconds to 1 minute or heat on the stove top over low heat until the butter is melted. Use kitchen twine to tie the chicken legs closed. Cut each garlic clove in half lengthwise, if using, and then cut slits in the skin of the breasts and thighs. Insert the garlic under the skin. Place the chicken breast-side down on the rack and brush the butter mixture all over it. Salt the surface and then liberally sprinkle it with pepper. Turn the chicken breast-side up and repeat with the butter, salt, and pepper. Lay the orange halves in the bottom of the pan.

3. Loosely tent a piece of aluminum foil over the chicken. Roast the chicken for 1 hour and 15 minutes, or until an instant-read thermometer inserted in the thigh and not touching bone registers 170°F and the breast registers 160°F. Transfer the chicken to a platter and let rest for 10 to 15 minutes, tented with foil, during which the temperature should rise another 5°F to 10°F.

4. Remove the twine and carve the chicken. Serve portions with the juice from the roasted oranges squeezed over the top.

Country Captain

This is a classic "low-country" dish from South Carolina. It incorporates curry powder, which some historians say became popular there in the 1930s when sea captains who had traveled the world brought back exotic spices to their families. A very Southern addition of peanuts adds a nice crunch. Serve this with hot rice and Mason-Dixon Cornbread (page 149) or Cheesy Yummy Baked Polenta (page 24). You'll significantly reduce your prep time if you use prediced onions and peppers, available in the refrigerated section of many produce departments.

HANDS-OFF: 45 MINUTES

SERVES 6

1 tablespoon vegetable oil

1 1/2 pounds boneless, skinless chicken thighs

Salt

Freshly ground black pepper

1/2 cup chicken broth

2 cups diced onions

2 cups diced red or green bell peppers

One 14 1/2-ounce can diced tomatoes

1 1/2 cups 1/2-inch-dice apple (1 medium apple)

1 tablespoon minced garlic

1 tablespoon curry powder

1 teaspoon dried thyme

6 tablespoons unsalted roasted peanuts

1. Preheat the oven to 350°F.

2. Rub the oil over the bottom of a 9 × 12–inch baking dish, then turn the chicken in the oil to coat. Sprinkle the chicken with salt and pepper.

3. In a large bowl, combine the broth, onions, peppers, tomatoes, apples, garlic, curry powder, thyme, 1 teaspoon salt, and 1/2 teaspoon pepper. Mix well, then pour the mixture over and around the chicken in the baking dish.

4. Bake, uncovered, for 45 minutes, or until the chicken is cooked through. Serve each piece of chicken with some of the sauce and garnish each serving with 1 tablespoon of the peanuts.

Grilled Salmon with Raspberry-Mustard Sauce

*F*resh raspberries add a bright pop of color and make an easy sauce for grilled salmon. I developed this recipe originally for a berry company, but changed it slightly to work as a hands-off recipe. You can substitute blackberries, if you like.

**HANDS-OFF:
18 MINUTES**

SERVES 6

1¹/₂ cups (6 ounces) fresh raspberries, divided
3 tablespoons whole-grain mustard
3 tablespoons olive oil, divided
2 tablespoons honey
¹/₄ teaspoon salt
¹/₄ teaspoon freshly ground black
   pepper
One 3-pound salmon fillet, pin
   bones removed

1. Light a hot indirect fire in a charcoal grill or preheat a gas grill to 400°F.

2. Reserve ¹/₂ cup of the berries. In a blender, combine the remaining berries with the mustard, 2 tablespoons of the oil, the honey, salt, and pepper. Blend until smooth. Pour half of the mixture into a bowl and reserve.

3. Brush the grill grate with the remaining oil. Brush the skinless side of the salmon with the remaining raspberry sauce and put it, skin-side down, on the grill.

4. Cover the grill and cook the salmon for 18 minutes, or until still slightly translucent in the center. Keep in mind that the thinner tail sections will be cooked all the way through.

5. Transfer the salmon to a platter and cut it into 6 serving pieces. Serve immediately with the reserved sauce, garnished with the reserved berries.

stove-top cuisine

One-Pan Chicken with Mustard-Cider Sauce

This is a great dish to serve in the fall, when fresh apple cider is available. Even though you're braising the chicken, it gets a nice brown color from the cider, making it look seared. Serve with rice and a green vegetable. Any leftover sauce is great as a sandwich spread!

**HANDS-OFF:
25 MINUTES**

SERVES 4

2 teaspoons vegetable oil

4 boneless, skinless chicken
   breasts

Salt

Freshly ground black pepper

1 1/2 cups apple cider

1 tablespoon apple cider vinegar

1 tablespoon whole-grain
   mustard

1 tablespoon cornstarch

1 teaspoon dried thyme

1 cup diced red onion

1. In a large skillet, heat the oil over medium-high heat until shimmering. Season the chicken with salt and pepper.

2. In a medium bowl, combine the cider, vinegar, mustard, cornstarch, thyme, 1/4 teaspoon salt, and 1/4 teaspoon pepper. Stir to blend.

3. Put the chicken in the hot pan, smooth-side down, scatter the onion over, and pour the cider mixture on top.

4. Cover the pan and reduce the heat to medium-low. Simmer for about 25 minutes, or until the chicken is cooked through. Serve immediately, with some of the sauce.

Stress Saver: If you use room-temperature cider, check the chicken after 15 minutes. Cold cider slows the cooking time somewhat (which can be helpful!).

Eye Appeal: Red onion adds a better color than white or yellow onion, but any of them will taste good.

Smoky Vegetable Chili

HANDS-OFF:
45 MINUTES

For New Year's Eve 2000, several friends and I hiked to a campsite in Pt. Reyes National Park north of San Francisco. My roommate and I made a vegetarian chili and trekked in a couple gallons of it! This is a similar recipe, using lots of different vegetables for a variety of textures and chipotles in adobo sauce for a hint of campfire smoke. Be sure to taste a bit of the chipotle before adding it to the chili, since the heat level can vary from can to can. Serve this with Mason-Dixon Cornbread (page 149), or if you're camping, just take along some good corn tortillas.

SERVES 8 TO 10

1 quart vegetable broth

1/4 cup yellow or white cornmeal

Two 15-ounce cans pinto or kidney
 beans, drained and rinsed

Two 14 1/2-ounce cans diced tomatoes

One 15 1/2-ounce can white or yellow
 hominy, drained

2 cups sliced zucchini or summer
 squash

1 cup diced bell pepper

1 cup diced red onion, plus extra for
 garnish

2 canned chipotle chiles in adobo
 sauce, minced

2 tablespoons olive oil

2 tablespoons chili powder

continues on next page

1. In a large pot, whisk together the broth and cornmeal until smooth. Add the beans, tomatoes, hominy, zucchini, bell pepper, onion, chipotles, oil, chili powder, garlic, cumin, oregano, and salt. Stir well to distribute the ingredients.

2. Set the pot lid ajar and turn the heat on to medium-low. Simmer for about 45 minutes, or until the onion and zucchini are tender and the chili is thick and flavorful. Serve portions garnished with extra onion, shredded cheese, and cilantro.

1 tablespoon minced garlic

2 teaspoons ground cumin

2 teaspoons dried oregano

2 teaspoons salt

Shredded Cheddar or Monterey
   jack cheese, for garnish

Chopped fresh cilantro, for garnish

Eye Appeal: Using yellow squash adds a nice bright color to the chili.

Vegetable Biryani (Indian Rice Pilaf)

Biryani *is a fragrant spiced rice dish that hails from India. It is often vegetarian (as this one is), but can also be made with chicken or lamb. Serve this as a main dish, topped with Raita (page 17), and some warm bread alongside. Or serve it as a side dish or as a bed for Chicken with Raisins and Almonds (page 132) or Tandoorish Chicken (page 109).*

**HANDS-OFF:
30 MINUTES**

**SERVES 4 AS AN ENTRÉE OR
8 AS A SIDE DISH**

3 cups vegetable or chicken broth

1 tablespoon unsalted butter

1 cup long-grain rice, such as basmati

1/2 cup sliced baby carrots

1/2 cup 1-inch pieces green beans or
   frozen cut green beans

1/2 cup frozen peas

1/2 cup diced onion

1/2 cup chopped fresh cilantro or
   parsley (optional)

1 1/2 teaspoons crushed ginger from a
   jar, or 1/2 teaspoon ground ginger

1 teaspoon minced garlic

1 teaspoon salt

1 teaspoon garam masala (see Note)

1 bay leaf

1/4 teaspoon freshly ground black
   pepper

1. In a large pot, combine the broth, butter, rice, carrots, beans, peas, onion, cilantro (if using), ginger, garlic, salt, garam masala, bay leaf, and pepper. Stir well to distribute the spices.

2. Turn the heat to medium-low, set the pot lid ajar, and simmer for about 30 minutes, or until the rice is tender but the vegetables are still slightly crisp. Serve immediately, or remove the pot from the heat and leave it covered to keep warm for up to 30 minutes.

Eye Appeal: Add 1 tablespoon toasted sliced almonds as a garnish to each serving for a nice texture contrast.

Note: Garam masala is an Indian spice mixture available in most large grocery stores. Or, you can substitute (for each teaspoon) 1/2 teaspoon ground coriander, 1/2 teaspoon ground cumin, and a dash each of ground cinnamon and cloves.

Grandma Martin's Swiss Steak

**HANDS-OFF:
1 HOUR
15 MINUTES**

I have a photocopy of this recipe from a seventies-era newspaper clipping on which my grandmother wrote "Good!" She used to make this for me a lot, since it was my favorite meal at the time, always accompanied by a variety of cut-up raw vegetables. This is a braised recipe, so it takes some time to cook the meat. Don't rush the process—just feed the kids and get them off to bed, then enjoy a leisurely dinner afterwards. Serve with some rice or couscous to soak up the tasty sweet-and-sour sauce.

SERVES 4 TO 6

1 1/2 to 2 pounds top round steak
  or rump roast, tenderized by the
  butcher if possible

1/2 cup all-purpose flour

1 1/2 teaspoons salt, divided

1 teaspoon freshly ground black pepper, divided

1 tablespoon olive oil

2 cups thinly sliced onions

One 14 1/2-ounce can stewed tomatoes

1 cup diced bell pepper

1 tablespoon minced garlic

1/4 cup Worcestershire sauce

2 teaspoons sugar

1 teaspoon dried thyme

1 bay leaf (optional)

Chopped fresh parsley, for garnish
  (optional)

1. To tenderize the meat yourself, pound it all over with a meat mallet or the side of a heavy skillet.

2. On a dinner plate, combine the flour, 1/2 teaspoon of the salt, and 1/2 teaspoon of the pepper. Press the meat into the flour mixture on both sides, coating it well. Discard any remaining flour.

3. Meanwhile, in a large sauté pan, heat the oil over medium-high heat until shimmering. Add the meat, onions, tomatoes, bell pepper, garlic, Worcestershire, sugar, thyme, the remaining 1 teaspoon salt, the remaining 1/2 teaspoon pepper, and the bay leaf (if using). Push the vegetables over and around the meat as evenly as possible.

4. Reduce the heat to low, cover, and simmer for 1 hour 15 minutes, or until the meat is tender. Cut the steak into portions and serve each with some of the sauce and a sprinkle of parsley, if desired.

Seafood and Chicken Paella

Paella is a Spanish dish that is probably the ancestor of the New Orleans classic jambalaya. It is flavored with saffron and paprika—specifically the smoked Spanish paprika called pimentón. If you can find this product, you'll be amazed at its depth of flavor. One of the hands-off tricks in this recipe is to use frozen shrimp, which helps to prevent them from overcooking. Serve this with Gazpacho (page 42) to start, or have a taste-off between the paella and Jambalaya (page 131).

SERVES 8

1½ cups long-grain white rice

2 tablespoons olive oil

1 cup diced onion

1 cup diced bell pepper

1 tablespoon minced garlic

1 pound tilapia or halibut fillets

8 ounces skinless chicken tenders or boneless, skinless breast

One 14½-ounce can diced tomatoes

½ cup sliced or chopped pitted olives

1½ teaspoons salt

1 teaspoon sweet or hot pimentón or paprika

continues on next page

1. In a large Dutch oven or other heavy pot over medium heat, combine the rice and oil and stir to coat the rice. Add the onion, bell pepper, and garlic and stir once or twice. Leave it to brown slightly.

2. Cut the tilapia and chicken into bite-sized pieces. Add them to the pot with the tomatoes, olives, salt, pimentón, and pepper. Stir the saffron into some of the broth to separate the strands, then pour it into the pot with the remaining broth. Stir well to distribute the ingredients. Put the shrimp on the top.

3. Cover the pot, reduce the heat to medium-low, and simmer the paella for about 30 minutes, or until the rice is al dente and the meat is tender. Take it off the heat and leave the pot covered for 10 minutes before serving. It may seem a bit brothy when the rice is tender, but the rice will continue to soak up liquid as it sits.

1/2 teaspoon freshly ground black pepper

1/4 teaspoon saffron threads

1 quart chicken or vegetable broth

12 ounces frozen peeled medium shrimp

Stress Saver: To prevent the rice from becoming overcooked, take it off the heat when it is still just a bit crunchy (al dente). Leave it covered or put a cloth on top of the pot for 10 minutes. The residual heat from the paella will finish cooking the rice.

Note: To use brown rice instead, add 1/2 cup extra broth and increase the cooking time to 40 minutes.

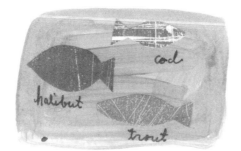

Pork Chops with Pearl Onions and Prunes

HANDS-OFF:
20 MINUTES

This is a classic German-French combination of pork and prunes, enhanced with aromatic herbes de Provence. *You can find this herb mixture in most spice aisles, but look for one with lavender included for a lovely floral addition to the sauce. Be careful not to overcook the chops or they will get tough. I like to serve this with Irish Soda Bread (page 153) to sop up the juices and braised greens for some added vegetables.*

SERVES 4

1 tablespoon olive oil

Four 8-ounce boneless pork
   loin chops

1/2 teaspoon salt, plus extra
   to taste

Freshly ground black pepper

One 10-ounce bag frozen
   pearl onions, or fresh pearl
   onions, peeled

1/2 cup chicken broth

2 tablespoons red wine
   vinegar

1 tablespoon honey

1 cup chopped pitted prunes

1 tablespoon herbes de
   Provence

1 tablespoon unsalted
   butter, diced

1. In a large sauté pan, heat the oil over medium-high heat until shimmering. Season the chops on both sides with salt and pepper. Add the chops to the pan in a single layer. Halve any onions larger than 1 inch diameter and arrange them around the chops.

2. Meanwhile, in a small bowl, mix together the broth, vinegar, honey, and the 1/2 teaspoon salt, stirring to dissolve the honey as much as possible. Add the prunes and herbes to the pan, scattering them over the chops. Put the butter on top, then pour on the broth mixture.

3. Set the pan lid ajar, reduce the heat to medium-low, and simmer for about 20 minutes, or until the pork is firm but still a bit pink in the center. Serve each chop pan-side up with some of the sauce, onions, and prunes. If you aren't serving all of the chops right away, remove them from the pan to prevent overcooking.

Stress Saver: If you warm the honey a little in the microwave or on the stove top, it will be easier to combine with the broth and vinegar.

Jambalaya

Jambalaya is a classic Creole dish of rice, tomatoes, and meat. I like using chicken thighs and andouille sausage for their rich flavor, but you could try other types of sausage or poultry. My friend Leslie likes to call this "Yumbalaya" because it's so tasty and makes great leftovers for lunch.

SERVES 4 TO 6

One 13-ounce package andouille
   or other smoked sausage,
   such as kielbasa
1 teaspoon olive oil
1 to 1¹/2 pounds boneless,
   skinless chicken thighs
1 quart chicken broth
One 8-ounce can tomato sauce
1¹/2 cups long-grain white rice
1¹/2 cups diced onions
³/4 cup diced red bell pepper
1¹/2 teaspoons dried thyme
1¹/2 teaspoons minced garlic
1 teaspoon salt
¹/2 teaspoon cayenne pepper

1. Cut the sausage into ¹/2-inch slices.

2. Pour the oil into a large pot. Add the sausage, chicken, broth, tomato sauce, rice, onions, bell pepper, thyme, garlic, salt, and cayenne. Stir to combine well and submerge the chicken in the liquid.

3. Set the pot over medium-low heat and set the lid ajar. Simmer for about 30 minutes, or until the rice is al dente and the chicken is cooked through. Take it off the heat and leave the pot covered for 10 minutes before serving. It may seem a bit brothy when the rice is tender, but the rice will continue to soak up liquid as it sits.

Stress Saver: To prevent the rice from becoming overcooked, take it off the heat when it is still just a bit crunchy (al dente). Leave it covered or put a cloth on top of the pot for 10 minutes. The residual heat from the jambalaya will finish cooking the rice.

Note: To use brown rice instead of white, add ¹/2 cup extra broth and increase the cooking time to 40 minutes.

Chicken with Raisins and Almonds (Butter Chicken)

HANDS-OFF:
30 MINUTES

This is an Indian recipe that my friend Alexei Rudolf and I developed to match a dish served at a restaurant in El Cerrito, California. It's a very flavorful but not too spicy stew, with the satisfying crunch of almonds and a touch of sweetness from raisins. You can add any number of colorful vegetables to this dish—3 cups of broccoli florets layed on top just at the end is a good choice. The saffron adds a distinctive aroma and flavor, but it's not essential. Serve with steamed rice and Raita (page 17).

Try to find Italian tomato paste in a tube and use it as directed to replace the paste in this recipe, or freeze any leftover paste from a can in an ice cube tray and store the cubes in a self-sealing plastic bag for recipes when you just need a tablespoon of tomato paste!

SERVES 6

2 pounds boneless, skinless chicken breasts, cut into bite-sized chunks

1/2 cup (1 stick) unsalted butter, melted

1/2 cup raisins

1 cup (4 ounces) slivered almonds, toasted (see page 151), divided

1 green serrano chile, seeded and minced

1/2 cup almond milk or whole milk

1/4 cup tomato paste

continues on next page

1. In a large pot, combine the chicken, butter, raisins, 1/2 cup of the almonds, the chile, milk, tomato paste, yogurt, garam masala, salt, cumin, turmeric, cayenne, pepper, and saffron. Stir well to combine the ingredients.

2. Reduce the heat to medium-low and set the lid slightly ajar. Cook for 30 minutes, or until the sauce is thickened and the chicken is tender. Serve each portion over rice, garnished with about 1 tablespoon of the remaining almonds and 1/3 cup of the tomato halves.

1/4 cup plain yogurt or sour
   cream

1 tablespoon garam masala (see
   Note, page 126)

1 1/2 teaspoons salt

1 teaspoon ground cumin

1/4 teaspoon ground turmeric

1/4 teaspoon cayenne pepper

Freshly ground black pepper, to
   taste

Pinch of saffron threads

2 cups cherry tomatoes, halved

Stress Saver: If your chicken is frozen, partially thaw it in the microwave. It will be easier to cut into chunks than if it were raw. The cooking time should be about the same.

Note: Almond "milk" is a nondairy product available in most grocery stores. Look for it in the natural foods or soy milk section.

Crista's Meatballs and Marinara

HANDS-OFF: 35 MINUTES

My sister, Crista, passed along a recipe for homemade marinara sauce that she likes to make for her family. Sometimes she adds fresh or frozen meatballs as well. Unfortunately, it takes 90 minutes to cook, so I wanted to see if I could speed up the process somewhat and make it more hands off. The recipe that resulted offers lots of variation on the hands-off theme: You can make everything from scratch (except the pasta), which takes 25 minutes, or you can use prepared sauce or meatballs, in which case the prep time is reduced to only 10 to 15 minutes. So choose the version that works best for you!

SERVES 6

Meatballs

1 pound ground meat, such as
   a mixture of beef and pork

¼ cup milk

¼ cup dried bread crumbs

2 tablespoons grated Parmesan cheese

2 tablespoons minced onion

½ teaspoon minced garlic

½ teaspoon salt

½ teaspoon dried oregano

1 tablespoon olive oil

1 pound dried pasta, such as fusilli,
   orecchiette, or spaghetti broken
   in half

continues on next page

1. To make the meatballs: In a medium bowl, combine the meat, milk, bread crumbs, cheese, onion, garlic, salt, and oregano. Mix well with your hands, but don't squash the meat.

2. In a large, wide pot, heat the oil over medium-high heat until shimmering. Loosely form a piece of the meat mixture into a 1-inch ball and drop into the oil. Repeat with the remaining meat mixture. You should have about 22 meatballs (or substitute 1 pound fresh or thawed frozen meatballs).

3. Add the pasta to the pot, but don't stir yet.

Sauce

One 8-ounce can tomato sauce

$1/2$ cup dry red wine

Two $14^1/2$-ounce cans diced tomatoes with garlic, basil, and
oregano

1 cup diced onion

1 tablespoon minced garlic

1 teaspoon sugar

1 teaspoon dried basil or oregano,
or 1 tablespoon minced fresh

1 teaspoon salt

$1/2$ teaspoon freshly ground black
pepper

3 cups water

Grated Parmesan cheese, for garnish

4. Add the tomato sauce, wine, tomatoes, onion, garlic, sugar, basil, salt, and pepper to the pot (or substitute one 28-ounce jar marinara). Add the water. Stir very gently on the top layer only, so as not to break up the meatballs.

5. Reduce the heat to medium-low, set the pot lid ajar, and simmer for about 35 minutes, or until the pasta is tender and the meatballs are cooked through. Immediately remove the pot from the heat and serve the pasta and meatballs with Parmesan for garnish. The sauce will thicken slightly as it cools.

Pan-Seared Salmon with Lemonade Sauce

This is a unique recipe in that you cook the salmon directly from the freezer. I learned the technique from working with the Alaska Seafood Marketing Institute, and it's an amazing discovery! A spatter screen is very helpful when adding the fish to the pan. Keep in mind that the thinner tail sections will cook more quickly; check them for doneness after 15 minutes. Serve this with couscous or Bread Salad (page 15) for a summertime treat.

HANDS-OFF: 20 MINUTES

SERVES 2 TO 4

1 tablespoon vegetable oil
Two 6- to 8-ounce frozen Alaska
   salmon fillets
Salt
1 tablespoon unsalted butter
3/4 teaspoon freshly ground black
   pepper
1/2 cup chicken broth
3 tablespoons lemonade concentrate

1. In a medium nonstick skillet, heat the oil over medium-high heat until shimmering.

2. Meanwhile, rinse any ice off the salmon with cold water and pat it dry. Sprinkle the flesh side with salt. Add the fillets to the pan, flesh-side down and at least 1 inch apart to allow for even cooking. Use the spatter screen now if you have one.

3. Add the butter and pepper to the pan, then the broth and lemonade. Tear off a strip of aluminum foil just wide enough to loosely cover the fish.

4. Reduce the heat to medium-low and simmer the salmon for about 20 minutes, or until it is still slightly translucent in the center. Turn the salmon over in the sauce to coat the other side, then cut each fillet in half for small portions or leave whole for larger portions. Spoon the sauce over each serving.

Ants Climbing a Tree

**HANDS-OFF:
20 MINUTES**

Isn't that an evocative title? I wish I had come up with it, but it's a translation of a Chinese dish that I first heard about from the late Barbara Tropp. The "ants" are pieces of ground pork climbing the "tree" of noodles. It's a really flavorful dish and a nice change for people who like pasta and meat sauce. Rice stick noodles are usually found in the Asian section of most large grocery stores or Asian markets. Serve this as a side dish with Roasted Asian Pesto Fish (page 97), or on its own.

**SERVES 4 TO 6 AS AN ENTRÉE OR
8 TO 10 AS A SIDE DISH**

About 1 pound ground pork (not sausage)

1/3 cup low-sodium soy sauce

1/4 cup rice wine or dry sherry

2 teaspoons cornstarch

1 quart chicken broth

1 tablespoon rice vinegar

1 tablespoon Vietnamese chili-garlic sauce
   (optional; see Note, page 89)

1 teaspoon toasted sesame oil

One 6- to 7-ounce package rice stick ver-
   micelli noodles (look for the nest shape)

1 cup sliced baby carrots

2/3 cup sliced scallions, including green
   parts

1 1/2 tablespoons crushed ginger from a jar

1 teaspoon sugar

1. In a medium bowl, mix together the pork, soy sauce, wine, and cornstarch. Set aside.

2. In a large pot, combine the broth, vinegar, chili-garlic sauce (if using), oil, noodles, carrots, scallions, ginger, and sugar. Stir in the pork, breaking it up well.

3. Set the pot over medium heat with the lid ajar and cook for about 20 minutes, or until the noodles are tender and the pork is cooked through. Break up the pork more, if needed, and serve immediately in bowls with plenty of the sauce from the pot.

Quick Cranberry Turkey

HANDS-OFF: 30 MINUTES

*I*f you like the leftovers from Thanksgiving best, then this is the recipe for you! You can make a quick cranberry sauce and turkey cutlets without having to roast a whole bird. I'm indebted to Rick Rodgers' book Thanksgiving 101 *for inspiring the sauce. You may be surprised at the amount of sugar, but keep in mind that cranberries are very sour on their own. You end up with a sweet and sour sauce, like a chutney. Serve this with green beans, Irish Soda Bread (page 153), and Better than Mom's Apple Pie (page 158) for the complete holiday experience.*

SERVES 4

1 tablespoon olive oil

Eight 1/2-inch-thick turkey cutlets (about 20 ounces total)

One 8-ounce bag fresh or frozen cranberries

3/4 cup sugar

1/3 cup chopped candied (crystallized) ginger

1/4 cup minced onion

1/2 teaspoon minced garlic

1/4 teaspoon ground cinnamon

1/2 teaspoon salt

1/4 teaspoon cayenne pepper

1 lemon, zested and juiced

1. In a large sauté pan, heat the oil over medium heat until shimmering. Add the turkey in one layer, if possible. Reduce the heat to low.

2. Meanwhile, in a medium bowl, pour in the cranberries and pick over them to remove any that are shriveled or dark. Add the sugar, ginger, onion, garlic, cinnamon, salt, cayenne, and lemon zest and juice. Stir well, then pour over the turkey.

3. Set the pan lid ajar and simmer the turkey for 20 minutes, or until it is cooked through and the sauce has thickened. Remove the pan from the heat and let it sit for 10 minutes for the sauce to thicken more. Squash some of the berries against the side of the pan to make the sauce smoother. Serve 2 cutlets for each portion, with about 1/2 cup sauce.

Hands-Off Technique: Adding the cutlets to the hot oil first allows them to brown while you prepare the rest of the ingredients, resulting in a more attractive dish.

Stress Saver: Zest the lemon before trying to juice it, or you'll have a tough time getting much zest.

Chicken Mole

HANDS-OFF: 30 MINUTES

Mole *(pronounced moh-lay) is a type of Mexican sauce based on chiles and nuts or seeds, and it usually takes hours to make. There are many kinds of mole, but the most popular in the United States seems to be the brown, or chocolate-infused, variety. It's not sweet by any means, but a bit of chocolate adds a depth of flavor to the mixture. You can greatly vary the spiciness of mole by the type of ground chile you use. Chipotle will be hotter; ancho or pasilla will be less spicy. Try using a combination for even better results. Serve this over rice or couscous with Chilled Avocado-Tomatillo Soup (page 43) to start.*

SERVES 6

One 14½-ounce can diced tomatoes

¼ cup dried cherries or raisins

2 tablespoons tahini (sesame paste) or almond butter

1 teaspoon minced garlic

1 tablespoon olive oil

2 pounds boneless, skinless chicken thighs

¼ cup (about 1 ounce) ground pure chile, such as chipotle, ancho, or pasilla (see Note)

½ cup fresh bread crumbs

continues on next page

1. In a food processor, purée the tomatoes, cherries, tahini, and garlic until smooth.

2. In a large sauté pan, heat the oil over medium-high heat until shimmering. Add the chicken, smooth-side down. Sprinkle the chile over the chicken.

3. Stir the bread crumbs, cocoa, sugar, salt, cinnamon, and cloves into the tomato mixture, then add it to the pan. Swirl the broth in the food processor to clean out the remaining tomato and pour that into the pan. Stir the liquid gently to combine it in the pan.

1 tablespoon unsweetened cocoa
    powder
1 tablespoon sugar
1 1/2 teaspoons salt
1 teaspoon ground cinnamon
1/4 teaspoon ground cloves
2 cups chicken broth
Sesame seeds, for garnish (optional)

4. Reduce the heat to medium-low and simmer the chicken, uncovered, for 30 minutes, or until it is cooked through. Stir and taste for seasoning. Serve each portion with some of the mole and a sprinkling of sesame seeds (if using).

Note: Be sure to buy ground pure chile, not chili powder. Most major spice brands package ground chile, or you can usually find it in the Mexican section of large groceries.

Thai Beef Curry

**HANDS-OFF:
30 MINUTES**

Thai curry comes in a variety of colors—red, yellow, or green—and is easily made using prepared curry pastes available in the Asian section of most supermarkets. My favorite is red curry paste, which goes well with beef or pork. The other ingredients that make this taste authentic are canned coconut milk and fish sauce. Even if you think you don't like fish sauce, you'll be amazed at how it boosts the flavor of this dish without making it taste fishy. So give it a try, and don't skimp!

SERVES 4

1 tablespoon olive or vegetable oil

8 to 12 ounces beef stew meat, cut
   into 1/2-inch pieces

1 red bell pepper

1 pound baby (new) yellow potatoes

1 cup sliced yellow onion

1 teaspoon minced garlic

One 13 1/2-ounce can coconut milk

1 to 2 teaspoons Thai red curry paste

3/4 cup beef or chicken broth

2 to 3 tablespoons fish sauce

continues on next page

1. In a large pot, heat the oil over medium heat until shimmering. Add the beef in a single layer and leave it to brown.

2. Meanwhile, seed the bell pepper, slice it thinly, and cut the potatoes into bite-sized pieces. Add them to the pot with the onion, garlic, and coconut milk. In a small bowl, stir the curry paste into the broth to dissolve it, then add to the pot with the fish sauce, lime juice, and sugar. Stir well.

3. Reduce the heat to medium-low and simmer the curry, uncovered, for about 30 minutes, or until the meat and potatoes are tender. Serve over rice or wide egg noodles, garnished with some peanuts.

1 tablespoon freshly squeezed lime
   juice
1 tablespoon sugar
Unsalted roasted peanuts, for garnish
   (optional)

Hands-Off Technique: Preheating the pot before adding the beef allows it to brown slightly while you're preparing the other ingredients.

Eye Appeal: Scatter some chopped fresh cilantro, basil, or mint over each serving for both color and flavor.

Chicken Paprikash

This is a satisfyingly saucy dish with a beautiful salmon color. It is Hungarian in origin, and therefore the paprika that you use is very important. Buy the best quality you can afford. I cheat sometimes and use the Spanish smoked paprika called pimentón because I love it so. This is perfectly delicious over egg noodles.

HANDS-OFF: 20 MINUTES

SERVES 4 TO 6

1 tablespoon olive oil

1 medium onion

1 red or green bell pepper, thinly sliced

1/4 cup Hungarian sweet paprika, or 3 tablespoons sweet pimentón (smoked Spanish paprika)

About 2 pounds boneless, skinless chicken breasts

1 1/2 teaspoons salt

Freshly ground black pepper

1 1/2 cups chicken broth

1/4 cup tomato paste

1 tablespoon honey

2 tablespoons all-purpose flour

2 teaspoons minced garlic

Dash of cayenne pepper

1/2 cup lite sour cream

1. In a large pot, heat the oil over medium-high heat until shimmering. Meanwhile, trim and halve the onion, then slice it thinly from stem to root end. Add the onion, bell pepper, and paprika to the pot and stir once or twice.

2. Cut the chicken crosswise into 1/2-inch strips. Add it to the pot and sprinkle it with the salt and a generous grinding of pepper. Add the broth, tomato paste, honey, flour, garlic, and cayenne and stir well to coat everything.

3. Cover the pot, reduce the heat to medium-low, and simmer for 20 minutes, or until the chicken is cooked through and the sauce is slightly thickened. Stir in the sour cream and serve the chicken and sauce over egg noodles.

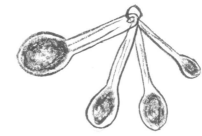

sweets & breads

Mason-Dixon Cornbread

I grew up near the Mason-Dixon line, which separated the North from the South during the Civil War. Southerners tend to like their cornbread with lots of cornmeal and no sugar. Northerners, on the other hand, like more flour and some sweetness. In the spirit of compromise, this cornbread has just a touch of flour and sugar, but mostly good, flavorful cornmeal and a moist texture.

SERVES 8 (OR 4 CORNBREAD LOVERS)

2 tablespoons unsalted butter

2 large eggs

2 cups buttermilk (see Note)

1 1/2 cups yellow cornmeal

1/2 cup all-purpose flour

2 tablespoons sugar

2 teaspoons baking powder

1 teaspoon baking soda

1 teaspoon salt

1. Preheat the oven to 400°F.

2. Put a 9-inch cast-iron skillet or a pie pan in the oven with the butter for just a few minutes.

3. In a large bowl, whisk the eggs to blend them, then whisk in the buttermilk, cornmeal, flour, sugar, baking powder, baking soda, and salt. Pour the batter over the melted butter in the hot pan.

4. Bake the cornbread for 25 minutes, or until the top is browned and springs back when touched lightly. Let rest for 10 minutes before you cut into wedges and serve while it's piping hot.

Note: Instead of buying liquid buttermilk, look for buttermilk powder in the baking section of grocery stores. It's a great ingredient to keep on hand for adding buttermilk to a recipe without worrying about leftovers. You can also use regular or soy milk in this recipe, which will cause the cornbread to form a thin and delicious custard layer in the center!

Savory Carrot Bread

HANDS-OFF:
1 HOUR
15 MINUTES

Carrot breads are usually sweet vegetable loaves, like zucchini bread. But I wanted a savory version with a texture more like a yeast bread, so I developed this one to make use of packaged shredded carrots. Of course, you can shred your own carrots, which will add more moisture to this bread. Practically any kind of nut would work in this, although sunflower seeds turn a bright green due to a chemical reaction in the dough! This is great smeared with cream cheese, and it's also a nice accompaniment to vegetable soups.

MAKES 1 LOAF

1 cup buttermilk (see Note, page 149)

4 tablespoons unsalted butter, melted

2 large eggs

1 tablespoon honey

4 to 5 cups whole-wheat flour, plus extra for kneading

2 teaspoons baking powder

1½ teaspoons Chinese five-spice powder

1 teaspoon salt

1 teaspoon baking soda

½ teaspoon dried dill

2 cups (8 ounces) shredded carrots

½ cup (2 ounces) pecan pieces or sunflower seeds, toasted (see Note)

1. Preheat the oven to 350°F. Line a baking sheet with parchment paper.

2. In the bowl of an electric mixer, combine the buttermilk, butter, eggs, and honey and beat on low speed until smooth.

3. In a medium bowl, combine 4 cups of the flour, the baking powder, five-spice, salt, baking soda, and dill. Stir with a whisk to blend. With the mixer on low speed, gradually add the dry ingredients to the wet ingredients, then beat in the carrots and nuts just until combined. Remove the bowl from the mixer and scrape down the sides of the bowl with a rubber spatula to incorporate the ingredients.

4. Turn the dough out onto a well-floured work surface and sprinkle it with ½ cup of the remaining flour. Knead the flour into it, adding more as needed, until the dough is barely sticky. On the prepared pan, shape

it into an oblong approximately 10 inches long, 5 inches wide, and no more than 2 inches high. Cut a large shallow X into the top with a sharp knife.

5. Bake the bread for 1 hour, or until it is browned and sounds hollow when tapped on the bottom. Transfer to a rack and let cool for at least 15 minutes before slicing.

Note: To toast nuts, spread them in a single layer on a rimmed baking sheet (jelly-roll pan) in a preheated 350°F oven. Bake for 8 to 10 minutes, or until they begin to be fragrant. Remove them from the sheet pan immediately, to prevent further toasting.

Applesauce Bread

HANDS-OFF: 55 MINUTES

A neighbor shared this recipe with me, and I liked how tender and flavorful the bread was without a lot of fat. Applesauce is often used in low-fat baking to replace some of the fat, but it also adds great flavor and moisture. Oat bran gives the loaves body and fiber without making them heavy. You can make these with any dried fruit, but I like the tartness of dried cherries or cranberries best.

MAKES 2 LOAVES

3 cups all-purpose flour
3 cups applesauce (about 27 ounces)
1 1/2 cups oat bran
1 cup packed light brown sugar
1 cup dried cherries or cranberries
1/2 cup vegetable oil
2 large eggs
4 teaspoons baking powder
2 teaspoons vanilla extract
1 teaspoon baking soda
1 teaspoon ground cinnamon
1/2 teaspoon salt
1/4 teaspoon ground nutmeg

1. Preheat the oven to 375°F. Spray two 9 × 5–inch loaf pans with nonstick cooking spray.

2. In a large bowl, whisk together the flour, applesauce, bran, sugar, cherries, oil, eggs, baking powder, vanilla, baking soda, cinnamon, salt, and nutmeg until well blended. Divide the batter evenly between the pans.

3. Bake the loaves for 45 minutes, or until they spring back when touched with a finger and a tester inserted in the center comes out clean. Let cool in the pans for 10 minutes, then unmold onto wire racks. Serve now, or let cool completely, wrap well, and store for up to 1 week. You could also wrap each loaf in foil, label it, and freeze it for up to 2 months. Thaw in the refrigerator before serving.

Eye Appeal: Sprinkle 2 tablespoons chopped nuts on top of each loaf before baking. The nuts will toast in the oven and add a nice crunch.

Irish Soda Bread

HANDS-OFF:
1 HOUR
5 MINUTES

One of the first restaurants I worked in was Kupchick's, a waterfront place in Lewes, Delaware. They always placed baskets of warm Irish soda bread on the tables as customers arrived. For a quick bread, it's really hearty and flavorful. Serve it spread with Charleston Chicken-Pecan Salad (page 19) for sandwiches, or with a stew or soup to sop up the savory juices. The recipe doubles easily.

MAKES 1 LOAF

2 1/2 cups all-purpose flour (divided), plus extra for kneading

2 cups whole-wheat flour

2 cups buttermilk (see Note, page 149)

1 tablespoon honey

2 teaspoons salt

1 teaspoon baking soda

1 teaspoon baking powder

1. Preheat the oven to 350°F. Line a baking sheet with parchment paper.

2. In a large bowl, stir together 2 cups of the all-purpose flour, the whole-wheat flour, buttermilk, honey, salt, baking soda, and baking powder until the flour is incorporated. The batter will be very sticky.

3. Scrape it out onto a well-floured work surface and sprinkle the remaining 1/2 cup all-purpose flour over the top. Knead the dough, working in the flour, until it is barely sticky. You may need to add a bit more flour.

4. Loosely form the dough into a 6- to 8-inch-diameter ball or oval on the baking sheet. Sprinkle with a little more flour and use the side of your hand to form a large X on the top, pressing down carefully.

5. Bake for 50 minutes, or until the bread is browned and sounds hollow when tapped on the bottom. Let cool on a wire rack for at least 15 minutes before slicing and serving.

Banana Bread

I love banana bread, and my freezer always has a few black-ripe bananas waiting to be baked into a moist loaf. This recipe was born of a combination of my two favorite banana breads, one from the Moosewood Cookbook and the one I made when I was a pastry cook at the Washington, D.C., restaurant Red Sage. It has a great banana flavor without the oiliness of many quick breads and the added flavor oomph of orange juice and zest. I like to sprinkle ground pecans on top so they get brown and toasty in the oven, but you can use other nuts or leave them off altogether.

MAKES 2 LOAVES

1¹/2 cups packed light brown sugar

1 cup (2 sticks) unsalted butter, melted

¹/2 cup nonfat plain or vanilla yogurt

4 large eggs

2 teaspoons vanilla extract

1 orange, zested and juiced

About 1 cup buttermilk

4 cups all-purpose flour, or substitute wheat germ for up to ¹/2 cup

1 teaspoon baking soda

continues on next page

1. Preheat the oven to 350°F. Spray two 9 × 5–inch loaf pans with nonstick cooking spray.

2. In the bowl of an electric mixer, combine the sugar, butter, yogurt, eggs, vanilla, and orange zest and beat on medium speed until smooth. Measure the orange juice and add enough buttermilk to equal 1¹/2 cups. Add to the bowl and beat just to combine.

3. In a medium bowl, combine the flour, baking soda, salt, and nutmeg. Stir with a whisk to blend. With the mixer on low speed, gradually beat in the dry ingredients, then the bananas, and mix just until blended. Finish mixing the

1 teaspoon salt

1/4 teaspoon ground nutmeg

2 cups well-mashed ripe bananas (about 3)

1/2 cup (2 ounces) finely ground pecans or sliced almonds (optional)

ingredients by hand, if necessary, using a rubber spatula to scrape the sides and bottom of the bowl. Divide the batter between the 2 pans. Top each pan with 1/4 cup of the nuts, if using.

4. Bake the breads for 50 minutes, or until they are light golden and a toothpick inserted in the center comes out clean. Let cool in the pans for 10 minutes, then unmold onto wire racks. Serve now, or let cool completely, wrap well, and store for up to 1 week. These also freeze well for up to 2 months, double-wrapped and labeled so you don't forget how long they've been there!

Leslie's Coffee Cake

My friend Leslie requested a recipe for a coffee cake that she could make on the weekend without having to leave the house for ingredients not typically on hand. This dense, moist cake is based on a childhood favorite of mine from The Betty Crocker Picture Cookbook (1956). If you keep baking supplies and frozen fruit on hand, you can have this for dessert or brunch in almost no time.

SERVES 8

3/4 cup sugar

3 tablespoons nonfat yogurt

2 tablespoons unsalted butter,
  softened

1 large egg

2 cups all-purpose flour,
  or 1 cup all-purpose and
    1 cup whole-wheat flour

2 teaspoons baking powder

1/2 teaspoon salt

1/2 cup milk

1 to 2 cups frozen berries or
  diced fruit

continues on next page

1. Preheat the oven to 375°F. Butter and flour a 9-inch baking dish or pie pan.

2. In the bowl of an electric mixer, combine the sugar, yogurt, and butter and beat on medium speed until smooth. Beat in the egg.

3. In a small bowl, combine the flour, baking powder, and salt. Stir with a whisk to blend. With the mixer on low speed, alternately add one-third of the dry ingredients and one-third of the milk to the yogurt mixture and beat just until blended. Stir in the fruit. Scrape the batter into the prepared pan and smooth the top.

Streusel

1/2 cup packed light or dark
brown sugar

1/3 cup all-purpose flour

4 tablespoons unsalted butter,
softened

1/2 teaspoon ground cinnamon

4. To make the streusel: In a small bowl or a food processor, combine the brown sugar, flour, butter, and cinnamon. Work the butter with your fingers or pulse it until it resembles crumbs. Scatter evenly over the batter.

5. Bake the cake for 45 minutes, or until the center is springy and the top is browned. Let cool for 10 minutes before cutting, or let cool completely, wrap well, and store for up to 1 week.

Better than Mom's Apple Pie

HANDS-OFF:
1 HOUR
15 MINUTES

If your mom makes pie as well as mine, then this might not really be better than hers. But it will undoubtedly be faster! The brown sugar in the filling and the butter from the streusel combine to make a caramel-like sauce around the apples. Try substituting other nuts for the walnuts, depending on what you have. The small amount of cayenne adds just a hint of heat to the filling. Don't leave it out—it's like the flavor of red hots!

SERVES 8

One 20-ounce bag sliced apples (about 5 cups)

1/2 cup packed light or dark brown sugar

1 tablespoon all-purpose flour

1 tablespoon water

1/4 teaspoon salt

1/4 teaspoon cayenne pepper

One 9-inch deep-dish pie shell, frozen or refrigerated

continues on next page

1. Preheat the oven to 350°F.

2. Pile the apples on a cutting board and coarsely chop them into approximately 1-inch pieces. In a large bowl, mix them with the sugar, flour, water, salt, and cayenne until well coated. Pour them into the cold pie shell.

3. To make the streusel: In a small bowl or a food processor, combine the walnuts, flour, sugar, butter, cinnamon, and salt. Work the butter with your fingers or pulse until it is the size of small peas. Pour the streusel over the top of the apples and pat it down lightly to meet the edges of the pie shell.

Streusel

1/2 cup (2 ounces) walnut pieces

1/2 cup all-purpose flour

1/4 cup packed light or dark brown
sugar

4 tablespoons cold unsalted butter,
diced

1 teaspoon ground cinnamon

1/4 teaspoon salt

4. Bake the pie for 1 hour, or until the crust is browned and the apples are tender. Allow it to rest for at least 15 minutes before cutting and serving.

Stress Saver: If there are cracks in the pastry, use a bit of water to soften the edges of the crack and then push them together. They should mend fairly well.

Chocolate-Mint Pudding Cake

HANDS-OFF: 45 MINUTES

This is based on a vintage-looking recipe card distributed by Ghirardelli Chocolate, probably from the sixties. It is amazingly quick to put together, and makes a very chocolatey cake with its own sauce. Dig in while it's hot!

SERVES 4 TO 6

1 cup all-purpose flour

1 cup sugar, divided

1/2 cup ground chocolate (see Note) or unsweetened cocoa powder, divided

1 1/2 teaspoons baking powder

1/2 teaspoon salt, divided

1/2 cup milk

2 tablespoons vegetable oil

1/2 teaspoon peppermint extract

1/2 teaspoon ground cinnamon

1 1/2 cups boiling water

1. Preheat the oven to 350°F. Spray a 2-quart baking dish with nonstick cooking spray.

2. Measure directly into the dish the flour, 1/3 cup of the sugar, 1/4 cup of the chocolate, the baking powder, and 1/4 teaspoon of the salt and stir with a whisk to combine. Stir in the milk, oil, and extract just until smooth.

3. In a small bowl, combine the remaining 2/3 cup sugar, 1/4 cup chocolate, and 1/4 teaspoon salt, along with the cinnamon. Stir with a whisk to blend. Sprinkle the mixture over the dish. Pour the water over the top, but don't stir.

4. Bake for 45 minutes, or until the top is set and the sides are bubbling. Serve immediately, in bowls.

Note: Ghirardelli makes a product labeled "ground chocolate" that is coarser than cocoa and has added sugar.

Kahlúa Cake

This really easy mocha cake is a tradition in my husband's family, and came from a friend of theirs. It's one of the first things that Bob made for me when we started dating. For a nice color contrast, try using white chocolate chips. Make sure to use a tube pan, as the cake won't bake as evenly in a regular pan.

MAKES ONE 9- TO 10-INCH BUNDT CAKE

One 19 1/2-ounce box chocolate cake mix with pudding

1 pint sour cream

1/2 to 1 cup Kahlúa or other coffee-flavored liqueur (amount depending on your fondness for coffee)

1/4 cup vegetable oil

2 large eggs

One 12-ounce bag chocolate or café au lait chips

1. Preheat the oven to 350°F. Grease and flour a 9- or 10-inch Bundt pan or other tube pan.

2. Using an electric mixer and a large bowl, prepare the cake mix using the sour cream, Kahlúa, oil, and eggs in place of the ingredients listed in the box instructions. Fold in the chocolate chips.

3. Spoon the batter into the prepared pan and smooth to make it fairly even. Bake for 1 hour, or until the top of the cake springs back. Let cool in the pan for 10 minutes, then unmold onto a plate or wire rack.

Eye Appeal: Lightly sift confectioners' sugar over the top of the cake for a pretty presentation.

Bourbon Street Bread Pudding

**HANDS-OFF:
1 HOUR**

This is based on a bread pudding served in a restaurant in New Orleans when my husband lived there. It has the classic Southern touch of pecans, with a more Northern addition of dried cranberries for color. The sugar on top adds a caramelized and crunchy layer. You only need about 1 pound of bread, but most good, crusty loaves come in 24-ounce sizes. Use the end pieces here and save a few of the big middle slices to use for sandwiches. This is delicious warm or cold, served alone or with caramel sauce. It would be a great finish after a New Orleans meal of Gumbo Rapide (page 34) and Jambalaya (page 131).

SERVES 8 TO 10

1 pound crusty bread (such as sourdough or sliced country white or potato bread)

3³/4 cups milk

¹/4 cup bourbon, whiskey, or more milk

3 tablespoons unsalted butter

1³/4 cups packed light brown sugar, divided

3 large eggs

continues on next page

1. Preheat the oven to 325°F.

2. Slice the bread into ¹/2-inch slices if necessary. Stack 4 or 5 slices high on a cutting board and use a serrated knife to cut into ³/4-inch cubes. Repeat with the remaining bread and put all of the cubes in a large bowl. Pour the milk and bourbon evenly over the top, stir briefly, and set aside. Add the butter to a 9 × 13–inch baking pan and place it in the oven to melt.

3. In another bowl, whisk together 1¹/2 cups of the sugar, the eggs, vanilla, and salt. Pour over the bread and fold in the cranberries and pecans.

1 tablespoon vanilla extract

1/2 teaspoon salt

1 cup dried cranberries

1 cup (4 ounces) pecans

4. Remove the pan from the oven and pour in the bread mixture. Press down the top to even it out and sprinkle the remaining 1/4 cup sugar over the top. Bake it for 45 to 50 minutes, or until browned on top and not liquid in the center. Let cool for at least 15 minutes before cutting.

Eye Appeal: The red cranberries add beautiful color, although other dried fruits work just as well.

Fruit Crisp

You can't get much faster for a homemade dessert than this versatile crisp. *Practically any fruit works well in this—fresh or frozen. I like to use pears, apricots, or mixed berries. If you do use berries, substitute white sugar for the brown in the filling.*

SERVES 4 TO 6

5 cups pitted or cored and sliced (if necessary) fresh or frozen fruit (about 2 pounds)

1/2 cup packed light brown sugar

2 tablespoons all-purpose flour

1/8 teaspoon ground cinnamon

Crisp Topping

1/2 cup old-fashioned rolled oatmeal

1/3 cup (1 1/2 ounces) unsalted nuts

1/4 cup packed light brown sugar

4 tablespoons cold unsalted butter, diced

2 tablespoons all-purpose flour

1/2 teaspoon ground cinnamon

1/4 teaspoon salt

1. Preheat the oven to 350°F.

2. In a large bowl, toss together the fruit, sugar, flour, and cinnamon until the fruit is well coated. Pour into a 9-inch pie plate or casserole.

3. In a small bowl or food processor, combine the oatmeal, nuts, sugar, butter, flour, cinnamon, and salt. Work the butter with your fingers or pulse just until the butter is pea sized. Sprinkle the topping evenly over the fruit.

4. Bake for 35 minutes, or until the crisp is bubbling and the topping is brown. Let cool for 10 to 15 minutes before serving warm, or let cool completely and serve at room temperature.

Amazing Coconut Pie

I've always loved coconut, and here it is in one of those magical desserts that separates into layers, making its own crust. It was originally from a biscuit mix company, I think, but it's much better made from scratch, as below. If you don't like coconut, just use all nuts. The filling ends up like a custard.

SERVES 8

2 cups milk

3/4 cup sugar

1/2 cup all-purpose flour

4 large eggs

4 tablespoons unsalted butter, melted

1 1/2 teaspoons vanilla extract

1/4 teaspoon baking powder

1/4 teaspoon salt

1 cup sweetened shredded coconut

1/2 cup (2 ounces) sliced almonds

1. Preheat the oven to 350°F. Spray a 9- or 10-inch pie pan with nonstick cooking spray.

2. In a blender, combine the milk, sugar, flour, eggs, butter, vanilla, baking powder, and salt. Blend until smooth. Pour into the pie pan and let stand for 5 minutes.

3. Sprinkle the coconut and almonds evenly over the top of the pie. Bake the pie for 35 to 40 minutes, or until the top is puffed and golden and only the center is still slightly wobbly. Remove from the oven and let cool completely before serving.

Beautiful (Not Just For) Summer Pudding

This is not an American custard pudding, but a British pudding—that is, a dessert. It is made of simply gorgeous purple layers of fresh berries and bread or cake that are weighted until the layers practically melt into each other. Of course, you don't need to wait until summer if you use frozen fruit; in fact, because it has more moisture, with frozen fruit you won't need to add as much juice. Serve big spoonfuls of this pudding with a dollop of whipped cream and a drizzle of raspberry liqueur.

SERVES 6 TO 8

10 cups (about 2¹/₂ pounds) fresh
   or frozen berries
1 pound challah or brioche bread,
   or one 10-inch angel food cake
³/₄ cup chopped fresh mint
1 orange, juiced
¹/₂ cup sugar (optional)
¹/₂ to 1 cup raspberry or blueberry
   juice
Confectioners' sugar, for garnish

1. Stem and quarter fresh strawberries, if using. Cut the bread into ¹/₂-inch slices.

2. In a large bowl, combine the berries, mint, and orange juice. If using fresh or unsweetened frozen berries, add the sugar. Toss and mash the berries against the side of the bowl until they are juicy. If they aren't surrounded by juice, then add ¹/₂ cup of the raspberry juice.

3. In a glass or ceramic 2-quart soufflé dish or bowl, place 1 layer of bread, tearing pieces to fit evenly. Spoon in one-third of the berry mixture and spread evenly. Repeat the layers twice more, then end with a final layer of bread.

Press down on the top with the back of a spoon to compact the layers. Pour any remaining juices from the bowl over the top layer or drizzle on some more raspberry juice until the top layer of bread is completely soaked.

4. Top the dish with a layer of waxed paper or plastic wrap and then a plate or bowl that fits just inside the dish. Put a weight on top, such as a bag of flour or two 28-ounce cans. Refrigerate the pudding for at least 8 hours for the layers to combine. Just before serving, dust the top generously with confectioners' sugar and then scoop out portions. Serve cold or at room temperature.

Brown Sugar Peach Cobbler

Brown sugar and peaches are a natural combination, and the cooked sugar turns into a caramel-like sauce around the fruit. Puffy biscuits float above the peaches and help to mark serving portions. Serve this warm, with some vanilla ice cream. If you have fresh peaches, reduce the cooking time to 35 minutes.

HANDS-OFF: 45 MINUTES

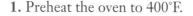

SERVES 6

2 pounds frozen chopped or sliced peaches

1 cup packed light or dark brown sugar, divided

1 teaspoon salt, divided

1/4 teaspoon ground nutmeg

1 1/2 cups all-purpose flour

1/2 cup milk

4 tablespoons unsalted butter, melted

1 teaspoon baking powder

1. Preheat the oven to 400°F.

2. In a large bowl, toss together the peaches, 1/2 cup of the sugar, 1/2 teaspoon of the salt, and the nutmeg. Spread the peaches in a 9 × 13–inch baking dish.

3. In a medium bowl, whisk together the flour, milk, the remaining 1/2 cup sugar, the butter, baking powder, and the remaining 1/2 teaspoon salt to blend. Spoon 6 evenly spaced dollops of biscuit batter over the peaches.

4. Bake the cobbler for 45 minutes, or until the fruit is bubbling and the biscuits are baked through, puffy, and golden brown. Let the cobbler cool slightly before serving.

Kir Royello

This is an adult gelatin dessert using the flavors of the classic cocktail kir royale. A kir is made of Champagne with a splash of cassis (black currant) or raspberry liqueur and a twist of lemon. Surprise your guests with a grown-up version of a favorite childhood dessert and save yourself some entertaining stress as well! You can use juice glasses, or sturdy stemware for a fancier presentation.

SERVES 6

One 6-ounce box raspberry gelatin
2 cups very hot or boiling water
1 lemon, zested
One 375-ml bottle Champagne, chilled
1 cup frozen or fresh raspberries

1. In a medium bowl, mix together the gelatin and water until the gelatin is dissolved. Stir in the zest and Champagne gently so as not to disperse all the bubbles. Divide the berries among six 8-ounce glasses. Pour the gelatin mixture on top.

2. Refrigerate the gelatin for at least 45 minutes, or until set. Wrap the glasses well with plastic if they will be refrigerated for longer than 1 day. These keep well for up to 1 week if wrapped.

Hands-Off Technique: Wrap the zested lemon loosely in plastic and use it as soon as possible for juice, so it doesn't dry out or mold.

Coconut Rice Pudding

My father loves rice pudding, so we ate a lot of it growing up. It requires almost constant stirring though, so I wanted to make a hands-off version. I substituted coconut milk for part of the liquid and added ground cardamom for a distinctive flavor. Use whichever dried fruit and nuts you like and have on hand. Serve this as the finish to an Indian meal of Aloo Cholay (page 54), Chicken with Raisins and Almonds (page 132), and Spinach Dal (page 52). It's also good left over, for breakfast!

SERVES 4

1 1/2 cups low-fat milk, plus extra
    for garnish (optional)
One 13 1/2-ounce can lite coconut
    milk
1 cup long-grain white rice
1/2 cup golden or dark raisins
1/2 cup (2 ounces) pistachios, toast-
    ed (see page 151) and chopped
    (optional)
1/3 cup sugar
1/2 teaspoon ground cinnamon
1/4 teaspoon salt
1/8 teaspoon ground cardamom

1. In a medium pot, stir together all the ingredients. Cover and set over medium-low heat.

2. Simmer the mixture for about 25 minutes, or until the rice is tender and the pudding is creamy. As it sits, it will absorb more liquid, so it should seem a bit wet when you turn off the heat. Serve immediately, with a bit of cold or warm milk drizzled on top.

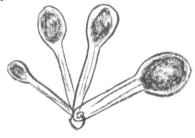

Wedding Ginger Cake

This is an incredibly delicious, moist cake that my friend Eric Shelton used when he made cupcakes for my wedding. He iced them with a Meyer lemon buttercream. Making this recipe as a cake is infinitely easier, and you can serve it plain or with a dollop of lemon curd on the side.

**HANDS-OFF:
40 MINUTES**

**MAKES ONE 10-INCH CAKE,
OR 12 CUPCAKES**

3/4 cup sugar

3/4 cup vegetable oil

3/4 cup molasses

2 tablespoons plus 2 teaspoons
crushed ginger from a jar

3/4 cup boiling or very hot
water

1 1/2 teaspoons baking soda

1 1/2 cups all-purpose flour

1/2 teaspoon ground cinnamon

1/2 teaspoon ground cloves

1/4 teaspoon freshly ground
black pepper

2 large eggs, lightly beaten

1. Preheat the oven to 350°F. Grease and flour a 10-inch round cake pan or pie plate or put cupcake papers in muffin pans.

2. In a large bowl, whisk together the sugar, oil, molasses, and ginger. In a small bowl, mix together the water and baking soda, add them to the ginger mixture, and stir. In another bowl, combine the flour, cinnamon, cloves, and pepper. Stir with a whisk to blend. Whisk the eggs into the ginger mixture, then stir in the dry ingredients until they are just combined. The batter will be thin—but this is okay! Pour it into the prepared pan, or fill the cupcake liners about two-thirds full.

3. Bake the ginger cake for 30 to 35 minutes, or until the top springs back. For cupcakes, check them after 20 minutes. Let cool in the pan(s) for 10 minutes, then unmold. Serve warm, or let cool completely and serve at room temperature.

Stress Saver: Measure the oil first, then pour the molasses into the same measuring cup. It will slide out easily from the oiled cup. If you want to double the recipe, use a 9 × 13–inch pan.

index

A

Almonds
    Amazing Coconut Pie, 165
    Banana Bread, 154–155
    Bistilla (Moroccan Meat Pie), 74–75
    Catalan Chicken, 102–103
    Chicken with Raisins and (Butter Chicken), 132–133
    Nutty Pumpkin Lasagna, 82
    Pomegranate-Almond Chicken, 98–99
    Romesco Sauce, 89
Almond butter
    Chicken Mole, 140–141
    Pomegranate-Almond Chicken, 98–99
Almond milk, 133
    Chicken with Raisins and Almonds (Butter Chicken), 132–133
Aloo Cholay (Chickpea-Potato Curry), 54
Amazing Coconut Pie, 165
Andouille sausage
    Jambalaya, 131
    Red Beans and, 46
Ants Climbing a Tree, 137
Apple(s)
    Baked Beans with Jalapeño and, 28
    -Carrot Soufflé, 25
    -Cheddar Quiche, 61
    Chutney, Pork Roast with, 105
    Country Captain, 118
    Maple Sausage-Stuffed, 26
    Pie, Better than Mom's, 158–159
Apple cider
    One-Pan Chicken with Mustard-Cider Sauce, 123

Applesauce Bread, 152
Asian cuisine
    Ants Climbing a Tree, 137
    Ceviche with Lime, 18
    Cucumber Salad, 13
    Peanutty Cabbage Rolls, 90–91
    Roasted Asian Pesto Fish, 97
    Spinach Dal, 52
    Thai Beef Curry, 142–143
Asian Pesto Fish, Roasted, 97
Asparagus Bread Pudding, Savory, 72–73
Avocado-Tomatillo Soup, Chilled, 43

B

The Back Porch restaurant, 21
Backyard Camp-Out Dinner, 100–101
Bacon
    Baked Polenta with Peppers and, 83
    Pea Soup Ann, 44–45
    Roasted German Potato Salad, 16
    Smoky Manhattan Clam Chowder, 55
Baked Beans with Apples and Jalapeño, 28
Baked Onions, Ratatouille-Stuffed, 94–95
Baked Polenta
    with Bacon and Peppers, 83
    Cheesy Yummy, 24
Baked Salmon in Puff Pastry (Coulibiac), 114–115
Banana Bread, 154–155
Barley and Beef Stew, 50–51
Batch preparation, 3
Bayless, Rick, 80

Beans
    Baked, with Apples and Jalapeño, 28
    black, in Pork Chili with Sweet Potatoes, 48–49
    green, in Vegetable Biryani, 126
    Italian, in Chicken Potpie, 66–67
    lima, in Brunswick Stew, 47
    Red, Andouille and, 46
    Smoky Vegetable Chili, 124–125
    Soup, Caribbean Black Bean, 37
Beautiful (Not Just For) Summer Pudding, 166–167
Beef
    and Barley Stew, 50–51
    Caramelized-Onion Brisket, 85
    Crista's Meatballs and Marinara, 134–135
    Curry, Thai, 142–143
    Egyptian Macaroni en Crema, 84
    Grandma Martin's Swiss Steak, 127
    Perfect Pot Roast, 106–107
    Texas Chili Meat Loaf, 86–87
Beer
    Beef and Barley Stew, 50–51
Beets
    Roasted Root Vegetables, 88
Bell peppers, *see* Pepper(s)
Berries. *See also* Cranberry(-ies)
    Beautiful (Not Just For) Summer Pudding, 166–167
    Kir Royello, 169
    Leslie's Coffee Cake, 156–157
    Raspberry-Mustard Sauce, Grilled Salmon with, 119
Better than Mom's Apple Pie, 158–159
The Betty Crocker Picture Cookbook, 156

Cooking/Quick & Easy

Get out of the kitchen, kick back, and relax—dinner will be ready and it will be great.

Hands-Off Cooking gives you more than 100 delicious recipes you can prepare in minutes and leave unattended. You can read the paper, catch up on e-mail, play with the kids, or entertain your guests while dinner cooks itself with no stirring, turning, or supervision. This will be your go-to cookbook for hectic weeknights or any time you want delicious, healthy food without the hassle. The recipes rely on fresh or high-quality prepared ingredients so you don't sacrifice nutrition. Full of recipes and tips for fuss-free, stress-free meals, this cookbook shows you how to put joy back into cooking. You get:

- ☑ More than 100 recipes, including salads and sides, soups and stews, savory pies and tarts, casseroles and roasts, stovetop cuisine, and sweets and breads

- ☑ Recommendations for ingredients to keep on hand and equipment and techniques that will save you time meal after meal

- ☑ Family favorites like Fridge Cleaning Frittata and Grandma Martin's Swiss Steak and special, impressive dishes like Seared Salmon with Lemonade Sauce, Ceviche with Lime, and Kir Royello

- ☑ Hands-off techniques and stress savers—tricks of the trade you'll use in all your cooking

With *Hands-Off Cooking,* you'll have time to enjoy yourself, your family, and your guests, and you're sure to enjoy a delicious dinner.

ann martin rolke is a culinary consultant in Sacramento, California, writing about food, developing recipes, teaching cooking classes, and editing cookbooks. She has cooked at several famous upscale restaurants, including Red Sage in Washington, D.C., and Mecca in San Francisco. Visit her Web site at **www.handsoffcooking.com**.

Cover Illustration: Beth Adams

Subscribe to our free Culinary eNewsletter at
www.wiley.com/enewsletters

Visit www.wiley.com/culinaryandhospitality

WILEY
wiley.com

BICENTENNIAL
1807
WILEY
2007
BICENTENNIAL

$17.95 USA/$21.99 CAN/£12.99 UK

ISBN 978-0-471-75681-1

51795

9 780471 756811